The ODELL BUCKENFLUSH CHRONICLES

Adding to the River Tales

STEVE SPENCER

DR. ODELL BUCKENFLUSH
"A LEGEND IN HIS OWN MIND"

The ODELL BUCKENFLUSH CHRONICLES

Adding to the River Tales

STEVE SPENCER

Wasteland Press
www.wastelandpress.net
Shelbyville, KY USA

The Odell Buckenflush Chronicles:
Adding to the River Tales
by Steve Spencer

First Printing – August 2016
ISBN: 978-1-68111-127-8
Edited by Jim Baker
Front cover photo: Center Rock Rapid
on the Cumberland River (Below the Falls)

Printed in the U.S.A.

0   1   2   3   4   5   6

DEDICATION

To my many friends in the
Ozark Mountain Paddlers

Your friendship and stories make it fun to write.

TABLE OF CONTENTS

FORWARD (STROKE):

What Are The Odell Buckenflush Chronicles?

The Odell Buckenflush Chronicles are a compilation of tales gathered from a career in the field of outdoor education. These tales illustrate the maxim that we should learn from our mistakes, laugh at our misfortune, and not repeat the same mistakes. While this compilation is not a treatise on learning theory, it does provide a variety of examples of learning. We all learn differently as the great American humorist, Will Rogers expressed:

"There are three kinds of (people):
Those that learn by reading.
The few who learn by observation.
The rest of them have to pee on the electric fence for themselves."

Throughout the Odell Buckenflush Chronicles experiential learning is mated with humor. Most of the tales have some type of learning parable which may be vague or blatantly obvious. While most of the tales have a humorous slant, they also have a moral or lesson directed at those who venture to the outdoors. Most of these tales unfold and decisions are made that have significant consequences.

Through the decisions we make, we develop judgment and learn from our experiences. As the great outdoor educator, Paul Petzoldt once noted, "People in outdoor settings should learn from their experiences, however many must have what 'just happened' explained to them, otherwise they keep making the same mistakes over and over." These tales are gleaned from a lifetime of good and bad river experiences. It has been said that "poor judgment" can produce some "good tales". If that be the case, then the Odell Buckenflush Chronicles has a wealth of examples.

The Odell Buckenflush Chronicles is a tool for both education and entertainment. After all, the educator is in the business of "edutainment." The Odell Buckenflush Chronicles address a life lived aware of our environmental impacts and consequences of actions in outdoor settings. The tales provide a source of fodder for Outdoor Leaders, Teachers, Camp Counselors and Resource Managers to utilize in an ever-shrinking outdoor environment.

Each Chronicle is divided into four chapters entitled:
1. Inventions and Achievements
2. Family Connections
3. Rescue and Survival
4. Philosophy and Life.

At the end of each tale is a segment entitled: "What really happened?" This part details the real-life inspiration of the tale. In the Appendix is located a "*Subject Index*" that further identifies which tales relate to specific areas of outdoor leadership.

Finally, there is no single person who is Dr. Odell Buckenflush. He is a combination of real folks, imagination, and folklore. Perhaps you may recognize yourself or your common experiences in some of these tales.

And...
Check out
Odellbuckenflush.com

PROLOGUE:

Origination of Rivers in Boston Mountains, Arkansas

In the Mountain Region of North Arkansas, a legend has been handed down for generations about how the rivers in that area originated. The particular Ozark mountain range is known as the Boston Mountains and five rivers originate within close proximity in this beautiful region: The Buffalo, the Kings, the White, the Mulberry and War Eagle Creek.

The legend originated with Native Americans and holds that a *red* star fell to earth in an area of Arkansas we now call the Boston Mountains. Where this star crashed, water sprang forth forming five different rivers. Early documentation of this legend may be found in old newspapers of Northwest Arkansas.

The falling star landed near what is now aptly known as Red Star, Arkansas, where one, Odell Buckenflush was born. Whether Odell was actually born in Red Star is debatable. He claims Red Star as his place of birth, but not necessarily during this lifetime.

As a lad, Odell began paddling in the rain-swollen creeks near Red Star. His first whitewater experience came on a wooden raft, built from some old whiskey barrel staves. He hauled the raft to upper War Eagle Creek and attempted his first descent on an unpaddleable section of water. His paddle, such as it was, consisted of a cut sycamore limb.

Young Odell was washed from his raft in the first drop, no more than fifty feet from the put-in. However, he crawled back upon the raft and continued, holding on for dear life sans sycamore limb, guiding the craft by shifting his weight to avoid disaster. Eventually, he maneuvered into a calm eddy, where he promptly tipped over. This tendency to survive the perilous while tipping over in the most simple has followed Dr. Odell Buckenflush throughout his life and has resulted in many a tale.

BUCKENFLUSH TALES CHARACTERS
(ALPHABETICAL ORDER)

Buckenflush Sr. (Odell's Dad)

Bezel Buckenflush (Odell's brother)

James David Buckenflush (Odell's cousin)

Jayrell Buckenflush (Odell's oldest Son)

Lulu Belle Buckenflush (Odell's Wife)

Mom Buckenflush (Odell's Mother)

Odell Buckenflush (Everyman!)

Tyrell Buckenflush (Odell's youngest Son)

Dr. Joe Giant (A big guy and Loyal Buckenflush companion)

Grandma Gibbons (Jon Nitrus' grandma)

Hosehead Grey (Jim Grey's wife and Loyal Buckenflush companion)

Jim Grey (Loyal Buckenflush companion)

Stu Hole (Loyal Buckenflush companion)

Jon Nitrus (Loyal Buckenflush companion)

Mike Oldnose (Loyal Buckenflush companion)

Auburn Redd (wife of Dead Ted Redd and Loyal Buckenflush companion)

Dead Ted Redd (Loyal Buckenflush companion)

Willy Joe Wiley (Odell's Father-in-law)

Willie Joe Wiley   Tyrell Buckenflush   Lulu Belle Buckenflush

Dead Ted Redd   Jon Nitrous

CHAPTER ONE:

Inventions and Achievements

BULL SLUICE MOOSE CALL

Anyone spending travel time with others usually invents ways to entertain themselves. The boredom that goes with long drives must be overcome in some way. Practical jokes, story-telling, and lies often lead the entertainment venue.

On a weeklong whitewater paddling trip in the southeast a few years ago, Dr. Odell Buckenflush and some of his compadres originated the Bull-Sluice-moose-call as a method of travel entertainment. This amusement came about when the group had taken out below Bull Sluice on Section Three of the Chatooga River. The Bull Sluice moose call was nothing more than blowing down the tube of an open Yakima roof rack usually just as someone was close to the opposite end of the tube. The volume was enhanced by the tube and always produced brain-scrambling laughter. Old-time hunters called their dogs in from the hunt using a similar technique with an empty shotgun barrel.

The Bull-Sluice-moose-calling fun continued throughout the week between paddling trips. Toward the end of the week the group found themselves in east Tennessee. They were near the home of Grandma Gibbons who had raised Jon Nitrus, one of their group. Jon suggested they stop by his grandmother's house for a home-cooked meal. The idea was warmly received as they were all tired from the travel, fast-food, and constant paddling. They needed a break.

During the past week, Jon had made several "scores" with the Bull-Sluice-moose-call. He did an outstanding job rattling the brains of whoever happened to be on the receiving end. With Jon's continual moose-calling, the group was starting to get somewhat jumpy. Prior to arriving at Grandma's house, a truce was declared and no more calls were to be made during the visit.

The visit to Grandma Gibbon's home was quite relaxing for the boaters. She was a very gracious hostess and she was the classic, petite Southern Belle, exhibiting a very gentle demeanor while aging very gracefully. Her coal black hair showed very little grey and her dress was the picture of perfection. She looked like she could have just stepped from the movie set of "*Gone with the Wind.*" If Grandma Gibbons had a flaw, it might have been that she seemed a little nervous around this group of boaters.

After a restful afternoon, Dr. B suggested they take Grandma Gibbons out for dinner. Being the gracious host that she was, however, she insisted on cooking and of course they all agreed. Who in their right mind would turn down a home-cooked meal?

After finishing the delicious dinner, the group prepared to head for another river. Jon and his Grandma strolled leisurely to the van while Dr. B was unlocked the van door. While saying good-by, Jon and his Grandma stood directly in front of the Yakima Moose call racks. Jon was carrying a large bag of leftovers which his Grandmother insisted he take. As noted previously, Grandma Gibbons was a rather small lady. So it was an honest mistake when Dr. B looked through the window of the van and saw only Jon (who had straightened out Dr. B's hair with the last moose-call prior to the truce). This seemed like a great opportunity to get even.

Dr. B bellowed forth a thunderous Bull Sluice moose call that echoed through most of east Tennessee! Jon had seen Dr. B prepare to call and the horrible realization of what was about to happen, dawned on him before he was able to act. Grandma Gibbons was totally at ease, enjoying fine conversation with her favorite grandson when the call blared near her ear. She screamed in horrific fright and jumped toward Jon knocking him backwards into a muddy ditch sending food a flying! When the rest of the group ran around the vehicle they found Grandma Gibbons astraddle Jon Nitrus, in the mud with food strewn everywhere!

The Bull Sluice moose call is still used by Dr. B and his boating friends though not around non-paddlers. Grandma Gibbon's coal black hair turned white overnight from the Bull Sluice moose call and she now resides in a nice retirement community where things are peaceful and quiet. Her twitch is now gone and she rarely demonstrates the jumpiness at unexpected noises that afflicted her for the past two years. She still sees Jon, but she won't allow any of his friends near her.

What inspired this tale?

The call through a Yakima roof rack with no end caps is real. I have been hit by this Bull Sluice moose call and have had the distinct pleasure of doing it to others. The Grandma Gibbons tale has some semblance of truth; up to the point my friend Jon saw me get ready to blow the call. He shook his head and I complied with a no blow, which was probably one of my better decisions.

ROPES–WHO NEEDS THEM?

Transporting boats during shuttles requires a good amount of knowledge of knots as well as common sense. Recent industry trends have been to market straps with a cinching device that can secure boats. The logic here is that the straps make for a better way to secure paddle craft while not leaving potential creases in boat hulls as ropes may do in extremely hot weather. While the use of straps is logical to a point, the need to understand knots and how to tie boats to car tops or trailers remains a basic skill that any paddler worth his salt will know how to do.

In the opinion of Dr. Odell Buckenflush, the increased use of these strap devices has caused a gradual loss of paddlers' ability to tie good knots. While the understanding of securing ones boat may be obvious, it often occurs along a learning curve. In his early paddling years Dr. B was always in a hurry to get to the fun part of any activity. As one might imagine, he tended to overlook obvious necessities, like securing a canoe during a shuttle.

The knot-tying experience that made quite an impression on young Dr. B occurred on a James River fishing trip in Southern Missouri. Odell and his brother, Bezel had decided to transport their canoe in the open bed of Dr. B's pickup. Neither brother had any rope to tie down the canoe but brother Bezel scrounged around and found some baling twine in the bed of the pickup. Unfortunately, it was pretty rotten and came apart when any knot was attempted. After discussing options, the two decided no ropes were needed. They decided that Dr. B, the heavier of the two brothers, would sit in the canoe in the bed of the pickup and hang on while Bezel drove.

With Bezel driving Dr. B's truck, the boys could leave right away and get to their destination, pronto! No need to wait on a third person to help with the shuttle because they could do this trip with one vehicle and save time. At trip's end Bezel would literally "run to the put-in" and drive the truck back to the take-out.

The first part of the trip went OK though Bezel had seldom driven a truck with a clutch and standard transmission. This resulted in a rather herky-jerky trip for Dr. B but he was able to hold on during the ride to the put-in. The fishing part of the river trip went fine. By the time they pulled into the take-out, the boys had caught enough goggle-eye and brownies for a good fried fish dinner. Now it was time for Bezel to run the shuttle. He put on his running shoes, which he had carried in his Missouri Dry Bag (5-gallon bucket) and ran back to the pickup. His running distance over the county roads was about six miles. Meanwhile, Dr. B waded and fished in the James River.

After finishing his run, Bezel drove the truck back to the take-out to get Dr. B and the canoe. The boys loaded up the canoe and their fishing gear and headed home with Dr. B again sitting in the canoe that rested in the pickup bed.

As Bezel reached the crest of the steep hill leaving the James River valley, he did a poor job shifting gears causing the truck to jerk severely. Dr. B was caught off guard as the boat flew out the back of the pickup with him in it! The canoe quickly headed down the hill with him hanging on for dear life. In spite of the threat to his existence, he was whooping and hollering the whole way. Eventually, the canoe hit a large rock and ejected him into a roadside mud puddle. Dr. B was fine though a little bruised and muddy. Unfortunately, the canoe was made of fiberglass and when it struck the rock, it had seen its last river trip.

The learning curve had been pretty steep this day as "experience can be a pretty brutal teacher;" however, the lesson was learned. The rationale for why one should *use rope to tie a boat when running a shuttle* was now obvious to young Dr. B.

What really happened?

There is *some* truth in this story. My first canoe was made of fiberglass. My brother Scott was a really good runner and for a while was the fastest high school sprinter in Southern Missouri. And I have seen canoes transported like this.

Knot tying is a skill that may not be as much of a necessity as it was in the past when transporting boats. The wide array of cinching straps has allowed those without knot-tying ability to successfully transport all types of water craft.

THE CANOE LUGE

Most people can relate to fantasies that feature themselves as Olympic competitors. These fantasies may be triggered every four years as the summer or Winter Olympics occur. A diverse variety of sporting events occur at each Olympics including new events that are introduced as demonstration sports.

Dr. Odell Buckenflush perceived himself as a potential Winter Olympic champion in the luge if only he had been provided with the correct training at a younger age. Regardless of training and age, Dr. B continued to sled whenever snow was on the ground near his southern home. The connection between sledding, canoeing, and the Olympics was a natural extension to a boater like Dr. B. During snowy winter, many a paddler has attempted to use their canoe, kayak, or raft as a sled. Dr. B chose to take canoe-sledding to the next level. His dream was to initiate a new Olympic demonstration sport: *The Canoe Luge.*

As the frequency of his snow sledding increased, Dr. B gained more confidence and skill in maneuvering his boat down progressively steeper hills. He was constantly looking for more challenging hills on which to practice this obsession. Eventually his sledding brought him to Lake Placid, New York, the site of past Winter Olympic competition and training center for erstwhile Winter Olympians. After considerable persuasion, which would have made any lawyer envious, Dr. B convinced the man controlling access to the luge track to allow him to use his canoe on the course.

On this momentous occasion, Dr. B and his ABS canoe were positioned at the top of the Olympic luge course. As he gazed down the luge run ahead of him, he had his first nervous misgivings about the intelligence of this endeavor. A gathering crowd was providing considerable encouragement and to back out now would be like the kid that climbs back down a high-dive ladder in fright. Putting his misgivings in the back of his mind, Dr. B shook off the butterflies, took a deep breath and pushed off in his Canoe Luge.

The boat rapidly gained speed in spite of banging the sidewalls while traveling down the course. Dr. B lost his paddle and hunched down as low as possible for protection. Eventually, the momentum of the steep course became too much. While rounding a curve, the canoe hopped the course wall and continued down the snow-covered hill with Dr. B hanging on for dear life!

At the bottom of the hill was a fenced sewage lagoon for the Lake Placid Olympic Village. As the runaway canoe sailed ever faster down the hill, Dr. B hung on precariously. At the bottom of the hill, the canoe hit a slight incline and the momentum took the boat airborne again, propelling it over the lagoon fence and plopping it right in the center of the lagoon! Miraculously, it stayed upright with one considerably dazed passenger.

A shaken Dr. B attempted to hand paddle and maneuver the boat toward the edge unaware of the large rotating arm that kept the lagoon water from freezing. It circled around and struck Dr. B square in the chest, knocking him backwards out of the boat and into the putrid-smelling sewage water! Eventually, he swam to the edge and pulled his boat out.

A very unique aroma accompanied Dr. B on his visit to the Lake Placid Infirmary for some well-needed shots. His Olympic aspirations in the Canoe Luge ended this day.

What really happened?

What do you think? Have you ever tried to control a canoe sledding down a hill?

BORDER CROSSING, SOUTH!

Paddling in another country is something that is on the bucket list of most paddlers. Getting to that other country destination often requires a border crossing and in some cases, multiple border crossings. The paddler who has completed the research knows what the expectations are prior to crossing the border.

The border crossing into Mexico from the United States is a pretty easy affair. One must have passport in hand and a legitimate reasons for travel but US dollars are appreciated in Mexico and in most cases the crossing into Mexico is an easy procedure. After all, the Mexican government did not build the fence separating the two countries.

When one comes back into the United States, it is usually more time consuming due to greater restrictions. One can expect searches and it is not unusual to see the drug dogs doing a thorough sniffing of all vehicles. All the "I's must be dotted and the T's crossed," when coming back into the United States from Mexico.

Dr. Odell Buckenflush and friends had been on a fantastic paddling trip in Baja California, Mexico. The two week sea kayaking trip in the Bay of Los Angeles had been a thoroughly enjoyable experience. The Mexico trippers had lucked out and it had rained just prior to their arrival. This had resulted in the cacti blooming, increasing the great beauty of the area. In fact, the group had enjoyed their time paddling in Mexico so much that they had elected to drive east on their return trip to the United States. They drove their van and kayak trailer through the Mexican states of Baja California-Norte, Sonora, Chihuahua, Nuevo Leon, and Tamaulipas; before they opted to cross back into the United States at the town of Progresso near Brownsville, Texas.

When crossing back into the USA, the crossing-protocol may vary, depending on the crossing point. On this particular trip, the Buckenflush group passed through the gate at Nuevo Progresso, Texas without any trouble. However, about 30 miles into the

United States there was another check station on Texas Highway 77. Dr. B noted that there were border patrol vehicles right next to the highway about two miles prior to all traffic stopping at the check point, which was in the middle of nowhere.

When Dr. B and company stopped at the border check station, they were greeted by a smiling border patrol agent who noted their kayak trailer and asked, "How was the paddling in Mexico?" They were making small talk about their kayaks when all at once they saw two guys start running for all they were worth across the flat Texas plains. Border patrol agents on ATV's took off immediately in hot pursuit of the obvious illegal aliens. The predictable result was a short run for the two "sprinters" who were rounded up and brought quickly to the check station.

Immediately, other members of the border patrol came to either side of the Buckenflush group's van with guns drawn! There was no nice small talk this time as the doors were wrenched open by the border patrol agents! All passengers were told in very rough language to put their hands behind their head and lie face down on the road. Then the border patrol agents went through the van and trailer with a fine tooth comb. But why? What had caused the drastic reaction?

It seems the two illegal alien sprinters had jumped <u>out of Dr. B's kayak trailer</u> where they were hiding! The Buckenflush group spent the next two hours convincing the border patrol agents that they were not smugglers of illegal aliens. They had no idea when or where the passengers had gotten into the trailer. After considerable warning and proof of their own citizenship, the Buckenflush crew was allowed to continue toward their Ozark homes.

As they pulled out after yet another border-crossing fiasco, Dr. B said, "Some fun, huh? I told you guys this trip would be a memorable bucket-list trip. Next time we ought to at least try to bring some Cuban cigars across."

What really happened?

This tale was inspired by a bucket list trip paddling in the Sea of Cortez out of the Bay of LA, Baja California, Mexico. It is truly a worthwhile Sea Kayaking experience. And seeing the desert cacti bloom after a recent rain is remarkable.

Crossing *into* Progresso, Mexico near Brownsville is no big deal. It does take a little longer *coming back* into the United States and you better have your passport. It takes longer to get through the highway traffic stop on Texas Highway 77 than crossing at the border. I did witness the border patrol agents hold a guy and thoroughly search his truck with drug dogs after they found something in his vehicle.

THE SOAP BOX CANOE

The canoeing industry continues to market new materials and unique inventions to boaters. With a wide variety of methods to propel craft continually being developed, it was only a matter of time before someone invented an amphibian canoe.

As a child, Dr. Odell Buckenflush had disassembled old tricycles and made his own soap box derby vehicle. He enjoyed coasting down hills in the craft until it was destroyed by the numerous oak trees that continually jumped in front of him. That enjoyable memory stayed with Dr. B and he eventually combined his childhood experiences with his favorite grownup outdoor activity, canoeing.

In a creative effort to merge both modes of travel, he decided to add wheels to his canoe. Dr. B disassembled two of his children's old tricycles and attached the small wheels onto axles that in turn were attached to the bottom of his canoe. He perceived his invention as a type of amphibian canoe that could be maneuvered somewhat like a large skateboard.

When it came time for the maiden voyage, Dr. B was living in St. Louis and chose a Mississippi River access with a smooth cement launching ramp. As his wife broke a bottle of Budweiser beer over the bow, the boat rolled gracefully into the Mississippi and off paddled Dr. B, proud and confident. The short test-run went smoothly down the Mississippi. As Dr. B prepared to disembark from his canoe, a couple of his friends arrived to congratulate him and assist in the take-out.

His companions pulled the canoe out of the water and pushed (rolled) the canoe, carrying Dr. B, toward the top of the take-out ramp that crested on a levee. Dr. B knew he had no brakes and was yelling for his friends to stop pushing as the contraption crested the levee. Upon reaching the top, the erstwhile friends let go and the amphibian canoe took off rapidly, heading downhill toward a busy road! To make matters worse, a tractor-trailer was bearing down at the precise place Dr. B and his craft would cross the road!

Just when it looked like Dr. B. would be paddling (and riding) for the last time, he deftly performed a duffek (hanging draw) stroke by dragging his paddle on the ramp, slightly turning the canoe which allowed it to pass safely under the tractor-trailer, barely in front of the rear tandem axle. Ever since that maiden voyage, Dr. B's amphibian canoe remained in the shed, except for the time his sons entered it in the Soap-Box Derby.

What really happened?

About the closest thing to truth in this tale is that as a kid I used a piece of slab wood and made a vehicle with wheels. However, I often think about following through on this design to make the portages easier. The influx of new strap-on-wheels for fishing kayaks definitely makes the portages easier.

HANDS-FREE ALPHA MALE

Fishermen have had hands-free control of bass boats for many years now. Trolling motors, controlled with foot pedals allow folks to fish without having to handle a steering wheel or to set their poles down. This invention has revolutionized the way folk's fish.

So what about fishing from a canoe? When bass boats were still being controlled with hand-controlled trolling motors, Willie Joe Wiley, the father-in-law of Dr. Odell Buckenflush invented a device that allowed for hands-free control while using his canoe. His invention preceded recently developed kayak fishing devices that have flooded the market.

Currently, the solo boating market has a number of devices allowing the fisherman to fish-hands-free. Almost all of these models are a version of a sit-on-top kayak. Some models utilize a bicycle type design and allow the fisherman to pedal their boat. Others use a rudder to control direction and apply velocity with the same foot controls. These are all great inventions. However, most all of these were preceded by Willie Joe Wiley's simple canoe controls.

Willie Joe never patented his invention so he never received credit for his ingenuity. He probably could have made some money had he developed the project in a different manner. However, he was always known as "the Liar's Liar" and his lack of credibility doomed him from receiving recognition for his invention.

Willie Joe's simple invention was ingenious. It allowed both the bow and stern canoers to fish hands-free. The stern paddler steered the canoe using foot pedals adapted from an old piano. These pedals allowed for ease of control and the canoe could be easily turned. Additionally, by applying the angled pedals in sequence, velocity could be added.

The invention was excellent when Willie Joe paddled by himself or with his wife. However, if he ever added his son-in-law Dr. B to the equation, problems were sure to follow. Dr. B continually snagged Willie Joe on his back-cast. Eventually Willie

Joe became disillusioned with the canoe control apparatus because of Dr. B's continual pleading to switch seats and his terrible back casts. The invention was controlled from the stern seat and there was *no way Willie Joe would give up the stern seat.* It seems there could be only one Alpha Male in the canoe and it was not going to be Dr. B.

What really happened?

This story was inspired by my wife's grandfather, Lloyd Horton. He invented and used a device similar to the one described in the tale above. He paddled all over the Ozarks in his 19-foot canoe with his pedal controls. The family has some great slide shows of his paddling the White River in Missouri and Arkansas prior to it being dammed to form lakes at Table Rock, Beaver, Norfork, and Bull Shoals. To my knowledge, he never *canoed* with his son-in-law.

EVERYBODY RIDES ABOVE THIS WHITEWATER

Shuttle drivers for river trips have a culture unique to themselves. While little documentation exists about this driving group, boating enthusiasts are all intimately aware of the connection between the shuttle driver and the paddler's experience on the river. Perhaps the time has come for social psychology to examine this unique group.

Probably the closest comparison to the shuttle driver would be the driver of a big-rig truck. The life of the big-rig truck driver is well documented through country music and movies with greasy-spoon truck stops, long-haul road hours, and the CB radio culture. As with most stereotypes, it is an exaggerated portrayal of certain characteristics. Truck drivers are as diverse as any other group of people and river shuttle drivers are most likely just as varied.

The common denominator among river shuttle drivers is *anyone* who will drive. A more accurate description is anyone who will dependably transport boats, people and gear. This leaves the possible personal characteristics wide open. In the case of Dr. Odell Buckenflush, shuttle driver extraordinaire, one trip produced the *nastiest label* a shuttle driver can have: "no-show".

The tale began as an ordinary river trip in early March. The temperature was warm and the water level was excellent for a section of the Wild and Scenic designated Obed River in central Tennessee. The paddling party traveled with a van and trailer carrying six people, boats, and gear. Dr. B was recovering from knee surgery and had agreed to run the shuttle, transporting his five friends: Jon Nitrus, Dead Ted Redd, Auburn Redd, Jim Grey and Hosehead Grey.

Dr. B dropped his friends at the put-in and spent much of the day reading and relaxing. His friends had repeatedly emphasized that he should be on time because they didn't have much daylight this time of the year. As it approached time to meet the paddlers at the Nemo take-out, Dr. B decided to make a quick rest-room break at a remote gas station.

Dr. B went into the men's room which had an outside entrance and took care of business. As he stood up and flushed the toilet his only set of keys fell out of his pocket and <u>into the whitewater that everybody rides above</u>! The keys surfed momentarily before being sucked down the drain to be seen no more! To make matters worse, the station owner had locked up and left for the evening. Dr. B was in a "pickle." He had thirty minutes to drive five miles and meet his paddling party on time. He had no spare keys, was in the middle of nowhere, and nighttime was fast approaching. On the plus side he was getting cellular service so he called home and reached his wife Lulu Belle. After a few minutes of begging and groveling by Dr. B, she agreed to make the 3-hour drive to the Obed with the extra set of keys.

About an hour later, a local farmer drove by on his tractor; pulling a tobacco trailer. Dr. B flagged him down and convinced the kind man to take him to his friends at the Nemo take-out. Two hours after the group had arrived at the Nemo takeout; Dr. B rode in on the tongue of a tobacco trailer, *without* the shuttle vehicle. A humble and chagrined Dr. B made his apologies to his paddling friends who rained a shower of abuse upon him. He said very little, allowing his friends the opportunity to "vent their respective spleens".

Two hours later, Lulu Belle Buckenflush arrived at the Nemo take-out *with the van*. She had brought the extra set of keys and Jayrell Buckenflush to drive the stranded van. There was no need for the "no-show shuttle driver" to drive home. Dr. B continued to apologize, trying to ease the hard feelings and eventually, a type of calm was restored among the group until Dr. B described the lost keys surfing better than any of his boating friends in the whitewater hole that everybody rides above.

What really happened?

This tale evolved from a combination of past paddling trips and assorted shuttles.

My wife has driven to the Obed-Emory River system to pick me up after I had vehicle problems on a paddle trip. As I remember, I hitchhiked to a nearby Cracker Barrel Restaurant to wait on her arrival. She stopped at three different central Tennessee Cracker Barrel Restaurants before she found me. It seems there is a Cracker Barrel at almost every exit on Interstate 40.

The lost key or misplaced key conundrum occurs regularly.

And I have served as shuttle bunny (driver) while recovering from knee surgery.

SHE-RAFT

River travelers have improvised with a wide variety of floatable craft throughout history. The improbable variety of craft and creativity to get on the water has also resulted in many boating failures. Rivers continue to be assaulted by folks coming up with new inventions and occasionally a successful new watercraft becomes a part of the river landscape.

During the time when Dr. Odell Buckenflush was residing in Kentucky, he and his friends often paddled the rivers of Central and East Tennessee. On a past river trip the friends had elected to paddle the West Fork of the Obey River in Tennessee. This is a pretty Cumberland Plateau stream that has some decent whitewater following a good rain. Accompanying Dr. B on this late spring trip was his cousin James David Buckenflush and Jon Nitrus. The trip resulted in a most memorable event thanks to a young man trying out an improvised paddle-raft.

The group was arriving near the take-out when they caught up to a teenager paddling a female inflatable doll. He was sitting astride the inflatable doll's belly and using a kayak paddle to negotiate the river. Though not making great time down the river, the young man was able to control his doll-raft.

The young man arrived at the takeout about the same time as Dr. B's group. Of course the doll-raft drew everyone's attention and Dr. B was dying to question the young man. Their conversation proceeded as follows:

Dr. B: "Do you paddle that doll often?"

Young man: Yes, absolutely, she loves to be paddled and I paddle her as often as I can! I call her my "she-raft."

Dr. B: "How does the she-raft handle?"

Young man: "She tends to be rather difficult to steer as she has rather soft chines with a pronounced rocker. In fact, sometimes she is off her rocker. At times I am certain I am paddling the correct line, when all of a sudden, the she-raft up and turns, taking a different route. And of course, her way is always the correct way. She is never wrong."

Dr. B: "Does the she-raft require any special maintenance?"

Young man: "Yes, at times the she-raft needs to be manicured to smooth out the rough places in her skin. The skid plate is a must for this model as she spends a lot of time on her back."

Dr. B: "Does the she-raft require any other special care?"

Young man: "When the she starts leaking, her hair goes under water. This is often because of bad air. A bad-air-day is also a bad-hair-day and causes me a lot of time, trouble, and expense."

Dr. B: "Does the she-raft leak often?"

Young man: "Yes, it seems every time I get to a point where I am comfortable, she springs a leak and I must spend more money on her. She makes me go both in debt and depth. It is a continual challenge to maintain my balance. I have a hard time keeping her head and mine above water for any length of time."

Dr. B: "Does the she-raft have any other drawbacks?"

Young man: "Yes, she tends to retain water at certain times of the month. At these times she tends to be a rather emotional craft, rejecting me for no obvious reason. When this happens, I can hardly touch her and it is difficult to keep us on an even keel."

Dr. B: "Have you ever had to be rescued when riding the she-raft?"

Young man: "Yes. One time I was unable to keep her full and happy and she struck her head on a rock. The resulting concussion caused a loss of stability and she sank into depression in mid-stream. I was afraid I had lost her. But mouth-to-mouth resuscitation revived her and we continued our happy journey."

Dr. B: "May I paddle your she-raft?"

Young man: "No! Absolutely not! The she-raft is "my baby" and she is custom made for me and me alone. We operate as a single unit. I am the only person who paddles her."

And with that, the young man threw the doll over his shoulder and headed to his car.

What really happened?

Thanks to my buddy Ted who was one of my early inspirations to write anything and have fun doing it. Ted saw a picture online of a kid riding an inflatable doll. It inspired him to write his own version of this tale.

THE VOYAGEUR

The old voyageurs that used to carry and transport furs were a very hardy lot. By today's standards the accomplishments of these men appear superhuman. The typical voyageur was usually small in stature resulting in more room in the canoe for the furs. More room for furs meant more money for the trading company.

Often these strong and compactly built voyageurs would transport numerous packs of furs at a time. This was accomplished through the use of a *tump line*-a band attached to the pack and then placed over the forehead of the voyageur. A single voyageur with the aid of multiple tump lines and a very strong neck might carry as many as seven packs weighing over 50 lbs. Each!

It has been said that "time is money." Another way the voyageurs increased the profits of their various trading companies was by transporting the packs of furs *quickly*. This was accomplished by paddling long distances and long days at high speeds. They further saved time by *running* with packs on portage trails when possible.

Dr. Odell Buckenflush perceived himself as a modern-day voyageur. He was of similar stature as the voyageurs described above and thought he had probably been a voyageur in a previous lifetime. He worked out, ran regularly, and was in good shape. He felt he could help others in his paddle party during portages by carrying more weight and by running the portage trails.

While this might seem like a kindhearted and worthwhile gesture, most folks prefer to care for their own gear and experience the portage. The great paddler/photographer Bill Mason, once said, "If anyone tells you portaging is fun, they are either lying or crazy." Even if the portage is a tough challenge, the paddler finishing a portage has a sense of accomplishment. The people Dr. B was paddling with did not "cotton" to his helping ways.

Dr. B had portaged the packs of his paddle group a couple of times and would run back to get his gear last. The third time he did this, his friends decided to teach Dr. B a lesson. While he was running the portage trail, they loaded an extra 15 pounds of rocks into his personal packs. As he was carrying his packs, he noted to his buddy Jon Nitrus that he felt a little weak and his pack felt heavy. Jon said nothing because it was his idea to load the rocks.

When the rest of the group arrived at the put-in following the portage, they found a pile of rocks next to Dr. B's packs. He was red-faced, breathing hard, and not in a very positive frame of mind. "You guys are messing with me!" cried an upset Dr. B.

At this obvious conclusion, Jon replied, "Anyone putting out as much energy as you was bound to eat more than his share of our food. We taught you a lesson for the good of the group.

What really happened?

This tale has occurred in multiple settings to many folks. I have had rocks placed in my packs and have placed rocks in other people's packs. And I have run a few portage trails; all when I was much younger and dumber.

PADDLE LA PIEU'

Nothing smells as refreshing as a clean river. But, because our vocabulary is limited, we often revert to describing rivers in terms of "water quality". Terms like: pollution-free, pure, fresh, sparkling, bubbling, and placid are more often used to describe rivers.

While terms describing the smell of good water may be limited, there is no lack of descriptors for anything foul smelling. In fact, many of these same colorful descriptions have been used when describing Dr. Odell Buckenflush's paddling skill. While his paddling skill has been much maligned, rarely have stinky descriptors been used to personally describe Dr. B. That all changed during a trip down the Nantahala River in North Carolina.

It was a very warm September day on the river. Dr. B, Dead Ted Redd, and Stu Hole were paddling and had arranged for Jon Nitrus to drive the shuttle. Jon was recovering from recent oral surgery and had suffered through a bad reaction to the anesthetic. While recovering, he agreed to serve as the "shuttle bun" (the male genre of the term: shuttle bunny).

The paddlers were playing at their first surfing hole when they noticed a nasty smell. The general assumption was that something had died nearby. In spite of the good play-spot, they decided to move on in hope of better air.

They paddled downriver and found another small hole in which to play. But immediately they realized the nasty smell was still with them. Perhaps it was the river that smelled? However, that was ruled out because the dam-controlled Nantahala watershed had little industry or cattle and few humans.

As they continued paddling, the smell seemed to follow them. The finger-pointing began because the stinker had to be someone in their group. The smell was worse than any polypro or wetsuit odor they had ever experienced. Eventually, Dr. B was identified as the culprit. Even he admitted he stunk, though he couldn't figure out why. The origin of the smell became apparent when Dr. B tipped his canoe while surfing. As he emptied the boat, the source of the nasty smell was revealed. A "ripe" dead possum was discovered under the boat's floatation bags!

Eventually, they learned Jon Nitrus had chosen to make his presence "smelled in his absence." While running the shuttle, Jon decided to take on additional duties, later described as possum mortician. To this end he had left his friends a little roadkill present for their river trip snugly wedged in Dr. B's canoe.

What really happened?

The evil trick with the opossum was performed by an unnamed friend.

In teaching students about camping and living in outdoor settings, hygiene is continually emphasized. The physical health of participants is obvious why this is necessary. The mental and emotional strain of being with an individual who smells bad in the back-country is something that can cause emotional, not to mention, nasal discomfort. I constantly emphasize washing and cleanliness. After all, as the actor, singer, and philosopher, Adam Sandler said, "No one wants to be the stinky kid in class."

THE LOANER BOAT

Most folks who live near a river will spend a lot of time on and around the water and will naturally find things left or lost by others – a treasure better known as "river booty". Sometimes finding the river booty becomes an adventure itself.

At one time Dr. Odell Buckenflush lived on the Finley River in Christian County, Missouri. During this period of his life, Dr. B spent considerable time on the river and found his share of "river booty." In one particular adventure, Dr. B was paddling and fishing the Finley with his friend, Stu Hole. This particular trip followed a pretty good rain that left the river running high.

About halfway through their trip the paddlers rounded a fairly swift bend in the river and came upon a strange riffle. Upon closer observation they saw an orange shadow just beneath the surface. The river was about two foot deep in a swift and narrow chute where the orange shadow appeared.

Being naturally curious, they decided to investigate further. After discussing the best way to check out this anomaly, they decided Dr. B would wade to the orange shadow (using a paddle for three points of contact). Stu had a throw rope ready, just in case of trouble. When Dr. B reached the orange shadow, he discovered it was a Coleman canoe, partially buried in gravel and lodged against a sunken tree.

After numerous attempts to dislodge the "river booty", they set up a Z-drag and eventually winched the canoe from its watery grave. Following a severe straining and stomping session, the boat was paddle-able, albeit somewhat crooked. The river salvagers decided to paddle solo for the remainder of the trip and Dr. B deftly maneuvered the beat-up Coleman to the take-out and hauled it home.

The crooked Coleman orange canoe remained in the Buckenflush fleet for about a decade. It was known as the "garbage boat" and was the boat of choice on many a river clean-up. But the best thing about the craft that resurrected from the river was that it was a good "loaner boat". It was especially good for those *not so close friends* that always want to borrow a canoe.

What really happened?

This tale was inspired when my buddy Stu and I found a Coleman Orange buried in gravel in the Finley River. We recovered it and stomped it back into shape so it could float. It was used as a loaner boat and trash boat in river clean-ups. It eventually was sold when I went back to graduate school.

PACKING OBSESSION

When it comes to pack-packing, the positioning of one's gear is an art. This tendency probably develops early in life when a child's mother tells the youngster to put his or her clothes away. Subsequently, the child throws the clothes in any container close at hand rather than placing them in a closet or drawer. Voila', the child's first pack-packing effort. The natural evolution of this scenario becomes packing the backpack or gear bag.

When it came to any kind of packing, whether for paddle trips or just plain packing your backpack, Dr. Odell Buckenflush always sought perfection. If not a perfectionist, he was definitely obsessed with packing the gear. Apparently, this zeal was formulated early in life and he has exhibited this obsessive-compulsive tendency ever since.

Dr. B always involved his boys in packing for family trips and his efforts were usually rewarded with various headaches. He usually brought much of the trouble on himself with unrealistic expectations. None of the Buckenflush family appreciated his packing enthusiasm. The boys just didn't have the same packing intensity as their old man. After all, few people in the world were as concerned with packing as Dr. B.

What could cause an individual to possess such a tendency toward packing gear? To find a clue, one might explore Dr. B's childhood. When young Odell was about 7 years old, his parents had arranged for him to go to a summer camp. The lad was very excited and decided to pack for the trip. Mom Buckenflush encouraged her boy and he quickly packed his socks in his bag before losing interest in the project (most 7-year old children have a short interest span, even the future Dr. B).

When young Odell arrived at camp and dug into his clothes, all he had was a backpack full of socks. For the next week, he wore the same clothes, but at least he had clean socks. That experience impacted the future Dr. B. and from that point on he always double-checked his gear and of course he always had plenty of socks.

What really happened?

This story was inspired by my brother Scott who ran away as a child and packed only socks for his adventure.

CHAPTER TWO:

Family Connections

THE FLYING FORTRESS
SLUICE

Most folks would agree that water quality deteriorates when vehicles are driven into and through creeks and rivers. Though possibly not a serious problem in many waterways, the attitude that encourages folks to drive vehicles into rivers should not in good conscious be encouraged. However, each year we see advertisements of four-wheel-drive vehicles driving through rivers. The protection of rivers continues to be a challenge and ignorance of environmental impacts is often the cause of such callous behavior.

In a time before his awareness of environmental responsibility and common sense, young Odell Buckenflush and some of his compatriots would drive automobiles through Ozark streams. This practice served no logical purpose. However, at the time it just seemed like the fun thing to do.

During one such adventure, a young whippersnapper, named Mike Oldnose *loaned* Dr. B his car. This was one big car that was known throughout four counties as the Flying Fortress. Some people called it a Buick, though to tell the truth it was some type of hybrid, salvaged from three different wrecks. The interior of the car was so large that when the back seat was removed, a Volkswagen could be rolled into the void. It was a great make-out vehicle. It was so large that Oldnose could take his entire homeroom and their dates to the drive-in theater, put them all in the trunk and get in on one ticket.

On the aforementioned adventurous summer day, Dr. B and company drove the Flying Fortress to a fairly heavily paddled river. Someone suggested he, "Jist drive right acrost the river to see if it could be done." The challenge was not ignored. With inner tubes, air mattresses and canoes all around, Dr. B goosed the Flying Fortress and it fairly leapt into the river! Spinning tires and belching smoke, it plowed into the water, leaving a fairly good assortment of river casualties in its wake.

All at once the Flying Fortress just "landed" smack dab in the middle of the river's current! Most of the riders jumped out through the vehicle's windows and tried to push it out of the river. As noted previously, this was no ordinary automobile. It wasn't called the Flying Fortress because it was made of balsa wood. No-sir-ree, it weighed in at about two tons. There was no way to move it as the waves began lapping up to about two inches beneath the windows. Things were looking serious when an armada of canoes rounded the bend and bore down on the Flying Fortress, which was stuck in the only passable route.

Dr. B's cousin, James David Buckenflush was still inside the behemoth because his window wouldn't roll down. In order for him to get out, he had to force his door open, which happened to be on the upstream side of the Flying Fortress. This resulted in a manmade sluice, which filled up the cab and sucked upstream paddlers and canoes into the back seat of the Flying Fortress! Just when it began to look like a phone booth stuffing contest, Dr. B opened the downstream door, flushing out canoes and water amid hoots and hollers.

Eventually the Flying Fortress was towed from the creek and the crew made their way home. Mike Oldnose's Flying Fortress was the talk of the Ozarks after that day on the river. Dr. B's river adventure had some other positive benefits. Oldnose got his car washed and received a free dinner when Dr. B gave him the 25-pound catfish that got tangled in the jumper cables under the back seat.

What really happened?

Parts of this story are actually true. The sluice happened in a Volkswagen beetle, not a large Buick when my buddy Mike forced the upstream door open. As I recall, no paddlers went through the sluice, but there was a definite sluice formed by the current going across all seats and something did get caught in the jumper cables. The flying fortress Buick did exist and was owned by my buddy Jim and reputedly provided for numerous friends' admission to the local drive-in theatres.

LOCKED, WHEN LOADED!

Paddling and camping go together like peanut butter and jelly. Driving to a river and then camping on that river or in nearby campgrounds is a common experience for many boaters. Additionally, most boaters are fatigued after a long day of paddling, so stopping to camp provides a safety net for tired drivers.

On a past river/camping trip in Tennessee, the Buckenflush clan had spent the day paddling on the Ocoee River. On their way home they planned to camp in the beautiful South Cumberland Recreation Area in one of their favorite sites at Collins Gulf.

The day on the river had gone pretty well. Dr. B actually stayed dry which according to him was about a 25% probability anytime he paddled the Ocoee in his canoe. Lulu Belle, Jayrell, and Tyrell rafted the Ocoee and had a great trip too. As they pulled into the Collins Gulf parking area they all agreed it had been a great day boating.

After the day paddling, all of the Buckenflush clan was dehydrated. They had been sipping on water, ice tea, and soda for a couple of hours as they drove toward the campsite. There was still a little daylight left when they parked, grabbed their tents and quickly headed to camp. On the short hike to the campground, they passed over a swiftly flowing creek and waterfall.

Running water effects most people in a very primal, anatomical way. As water flows it makes a noise to which we all can all relate. And that urge to purge (ones bladder) usually follows. The Buckenflush Clan was usually the first to visit a restroom when nature called. Dr. B and the boys were always hydrating (sipping on a soda) during their travels which only added to this tendency. However, with Lulu Belle Buckenflush, it was even money that she would be the first to visit any available restroom facility once the vehicle stopped moving.

Upon arriving at the campsite, Lulu Belle made her normal beeline for the nearest privy while the boys set up the tents. The privies in the South Cumberland Natural Area are an improved version of an outhouse that prevents bears and other varmints from getting into the toilets. The improvement consisted of a pivoting knob on the *outside* of the door. Having barely made it to her throne, a loaded Lulu Belle dropped her shorts and took care of business. Now she was relieved and all was right with the world.

The outhouse Lulu Belle had selected was about 60 yards from their campsite. Dr. B and the boys were exhausted and had taken care of their bladder business on the short hike to the campsite. All three set up tents and were asleep in minutes. Meanwhile, in her hast to reach the toilet, Lulu Belle slammed the door and the outside latch slid into place, locking her inside. Her attempts to open the door were curtailed when she realized there was a wasp nest at the inside top of the door and the wasps were getting a bit riled up. To make matters worse, she was a long way from her family and at that moment there was nobody else in the campground!

What to do? Lulu Belle could not shake the door due to the wasp nest. She could not open the door due to the outside latch. Her only alternative was to holler for help. And holler she did! She started off with a rather pleading cry for her husband who was asleep. She hollered for her boys who were also asleep. She hollered for anyone, all to no avail! Eventually the slumbering Dr. B heard a loud cry of his name, followed by a few cuss words. Following the sound of his wife's cries, Dr. B rescued Lulu Belle from the outhouse and all was copasetic with the world.

What really happened?

This tale was based on a similar event involving my wife. Deb did get locked in the outhouse at Collins West primitive campsite in The South Cumberland Natural Area and there was a wasp nest at the top of the outhouse door. She and I were the only ones in the camping area. Eventually, I heard her cries (no actual cussing) and opened the door and we avoided the wasps. We used the woods for the remainder of our trip.

The part about staying dry 25% of the time when paddling the Ocoee is about right for me.

FINLEY RIVER BAPTISM

For years, the code of folks living in river valleys in this country was: "The answer to pollution is dilution." But as our country has become more aware of environmental limits and the necessity for clean water, the slogan has become: "We all live downstream."

During Dr. Odell Buckenflush's early years as a parent he lived on the banks of the Finley River in Missouri's Ozark mountain area. This was a steep learning curve period of his life as he moved into the real world of adulthood, marriage, supporting a family, owning a home, and parenthood. This was also a time before he became more environmentally aware of his individual responsibilities and he did a few things that were less than environmentally sound. While not severe on the environmental degradation scale, it was closer to the early philosophy of, "the answer to pollution is dilution".

Having always had a rather weak stomach, Dr. B was the type of guy that if someone started talking about vomit, he usually got sick. If he ever saw a person vomit, it was not too long until he was vomiting too. One time he even went into a type of shock when he saw his own blood. This is known as psycho-genic shock and while not serious, it can lead to people fainting when they see something traumatic. Later in life, when he taught in the Wilderness First Responder program he referred to this occurrence as Wimp-ogenic Shock.

Once parenthood happened, Dr. B found himself having to change diapers. Because he was such a wimp and always gagging around baby poop, his wife, Lulu Belle found it easier to clean the boys herself rather than put up with Dr. B being such a big baby. This was fine with Dr. B. He rationalized this behavior as *very smart* on his part. After all, he did not have to change diapers and avoided getting sick.

Of course there were times when Lulu Belle was not around to help and the inevitable (poop) happened. In times such as these, Dr. B would go visit the river with the necessary child. Being the grandson of a Baptist minister, Dr. B had witnessed a few river baptisms and occasionally did a quick baptismal dip with dirty boy to clean him up. Dr. B justified this action as a kind of spiritual as well as physical cleansing of his children.

In this situation the answer to the Buckenflush kid's pollution was Finley River dilution.

What really happened?

This story has a lot of truth in it. I confess. I occasionally did this with my boys, especially when they were real messy. I further confess that the water temperature rarely mattered when this took place. I have done many river cleanups and continue to monitor water quality in streams as a type of penance.

HANGIN' WITH THE
BUCKENFLUSHES

Take a deep hole in the river with a large tree nearby. Add a supply of imagination with some rope and you have now created that great river entertainment- the rope swing. Every person who has ever traveled a river has seen a rope swing and most people have tried them at one time or another. Rope swings are a standard part of our American river culture.

The Buckenflush family has been a part of that American river culture for many years and they were always avid rope-swingers. They had a family pact whereby they would never pass a rope swing without someone giving it a try. This was a long-standing tradition, which endured for years despite numerous near catastrophes.

The Buckenflush children were the most devoted enthusiasts of this tradition. Both Jayrell and Tyrell had grown up rope-swinging and had survived to date. Each had become proficient with varying technique. Though not up to Olympic caliber, they could flip with the best if the conditions were right.

One day the Buckenflush's decided to take a family trip down Drakes Creek in Southern Kentucky. It was a glorious warm summer day and the river level was perfect. Jayrell and Tyrell were paddling together while Lulu Belle and Dr. B lazily brought up the rear. The Buckenflush boys had put considerable distance between themselves and their parents.

As the adults rounded a bend in the river, the quiet reverie of the peaceful stream was disturbed by loud cries of distress, immediately followed by gales of laughter! Dr. B and Lulu Belle picked up their pace, curious to discover the cause of the commotion. Once they were in viewing distance, they beheld Jayrell rolling in laughter on a gravel bar. Nowhere was young Tyrell to be seen. Dr. B asked his older son the obvious question, "Where's Tyrell?" Without saying a word, the older Buckenflush youth pointed up to a spot in the trees. There was Tyrell, hanging from a limb by the seat of his pants!

He had snagged his pants on the limb as he was attempting to get some height after letting go of the rope swing. Rather than breaking, the limb was flexible enough and Tyrell was light enough to just "hang-out."

Eventually, Jayrell brought the rope close enough where Tyrell could latch onto it. He then finished his jump and landed in the river, but not before Dr. B had some classic pictures.

What really happened?

This tale was inspired by an event when my boys were pretty young. My oldest son, Beau, came running up to our home one day yelling, "Grab the camera! Grab the camera!" When asked what the commotion was about, he laughingly said, "You have to come and see this, RIGHT NOW!" We all ran down toward a large hickory tree that the boys had been climbing. My youngest son, Ty, had fallen from a higher limb and actually snagged his pants on a lower tree limb. He never hit ground and was hanging by the seat of his pants above the ground, giggling and gently swaying up and down.

BRACING ON THE DROP

Keeping paddling gear clean is a necessity that is often neglected by active boaters. While it can be a real challenge, conscientious maintenance will assure equipment lasts for years. If a boater is fortunate enough to live close enough to water and have laundry service, then it is a real nice perk.

Early during their marriage, Dr. Odell and Lulu Belle Buckenflush lived adjacent to a river they paddled quite frequently. In fact they spent so much time in the river that it seemed their family's clothes were always wet and in need of washing. Lulu Belle, as nurturing wife took this duty upon herself.

In their home, the laundry area was in the basement. In one of her creative inspirations, Lulu Belle decided to make a laundry chute into the basement. To build this laundry chute, she cut a hole in the floor while Dr. B was at work. She had failed to thoroughly think this construction event through. The result of her plan left the laundry chute (hole she had cut) at the *opposite end of the basement* from where the washer and dryer were located. After realizing her mistake she decided, "If you are going to do something; then do it right." In order for her to do it right, she went to the correct end of the house and proceeded to cut the hole (her laundry chute) in the correct location. She put a little box laundry hamper with the bottom cut out of it over the new hole and it worked fine.

But what about the other hole in the floor? In her haste to complete her project, she had put a rug over the hole and forgot about it. The first hole was in an unused bedroom where she and Dr. B kept their camping, fishing, hunting, and boating gear.

As fate would have it, Dr. B came home and wanted to go canoeing. He went into the gear room and grabbed his paddle and life jacket and was headed out the door. (You all know what is going to happen next). Of course Dr. B stepped on the rug-covered hole and promptly became laundry at the wrong end of the basement! He fell through the hole, yelled some very polite terms, bounced on some boxes, and landed in a cardboard footlocker with his feet up in the air and paddle still in hand!

When Lulu Belle heard the commotion, she immediately knew what had happened. She ran down stairs and found Dr. B still lying in the cardboard footlocker, feet up in the air with his paddle in hand. Being not the least bit dazed or confused, his first comment was, "I seemed to have missed my low brace on that hole."

What really happened?

This tale was inspired by my mother-in-law, Sally who actually did cut a hole in the floor of their home for a laundry chute only to discover the washer and dryer were at the other end of the basement. To my knowledge, nobody fell through the hole.

DO IT AGAIN, DADDY

Running shuttles for paddling trips continues to be a source of considerable variety. Any number of possible means may be utilized as a way to get boaters and gear together after the trip is over. Shuttles are limited only by one's imagination.

A few years back, Dr. Odell Buckenflush had planned a family paddling trip in the Missouri Ozarks on the Finley River. He and wife Lulu Belle were going canoeing with their two small children (ages three and five). They decided each parent would drive a vehicle to complete the shuttle. Dr. B had a pretty good knowledge of the area and the river route was one he had paddled before.

The day of the trip arrived and a "wrench was thrown into the works" when Lulu Belle was called into work. Dr. B and the boys had been looking forward to the river trip and a decision had to be made regarding *how or if* the river trip would still continue. After a bit of 'shuttle-diplomacy" with his wife, Dr. B decided to take his old ten-speed bicycle and "ride" the shuttle by hauling the children in his two-child bike trailer. The bicycle and trailer could be hauled in his truck and locked up at the take-out. Dr. B then drove his truck with the canoe and his children back to the put-in where they began the canoe trip.

The river trip down the Finley was enjoyable and the boys spent a lot of time swimming, skipping rocks and catching crawdads. In fact, the time spent out of the canoe was greater than the time spent in the canoe. By the time Dr. B and his two boys arrived at the takeout, they were all three exhausted from a great day on the river.

Dr. B pulled the canoe to a nearby tree and secured it and the paddling gear. Now came time for the shuttle. Though he was tired from paddling, he was looking forward to the trip with the children. Putting each child in a helmet and strapping both in the trailer, Dr. and the boys took off via the road for the put-in where he had left his truck.

It is interesting how driving a route can be so different from walking and/or biking the same route. So it was on this day. The hills which seemed so minor were suddenly much steeper and longer when riding a bicycle with an attached trailer over the route. As Dr. B headed down the steepest and last hill toward the put-in he was forced to brake repeatedly on his old ten-speed. To make matters worse, the dirt road had deep washboard ruts.

The combination of downhill momentum, slick dirt surface and washboard nature of the roads combined with the bad brakes of the 10-speed caused the trailer to fish-tail out from behind the bike! The trailer hit a large rock and came up on one wheel and almost tipped over before slamming back down! Oblivious to what was an extremely dangerous situation the Buckenflush boys were hooting, hollering and "having a blast!" There was a continuous screaming chant of, "Do it again, Daddy!" as Dr. B struggled for control of the run-away bike trailer.

Finally control of the bike and trailer was regained by Dr. B who quickly stopped, unstrapped and hugged his boys tight.

The next day he bought a mountain bike with great brakes.

What really happened?

This story was inspired by biking and pulling child-trailers around Ozark roads. I remember riding the Fayetteville, Arkansas hills when I almost tipped a trailer carrying my two boys on a downhill stretch. They were riding behind my old Peugeot 10-speed bike and the brakes were too weak for the load. A trailer wheel hit a curb and tipped up onto one wheel for what seemed like an eternity before slamming down amid their hoots of laughter.

With this and other near misses, it is truly a wonder that our children survived childhood.

AMPHIBIAN ENEMA

Most children have an affinity for wild things. This love of wild creatures whether reptile, insect or animals may continue throughout life. However, the love of the wild may just as often turn to fear during an early stage of a child's development. That fear may result from some twisted horror show that made a lasting impression on the young and impressionable psyche or, more often than not, may be the result of some well-meaning adult imposing some obtuse parenting method on the child.

Both sides of the affinity/fear syndrome were in evidence with Dr. Odell Buckenflush and his son, Tyrell. Young Tyrell had always exhibited an interest in things wild, especially frogs and toads. He was constantly catching the amphibians and playing with them before letting them go. His parents had worked with him and his elder brother in fostering a deep respect for all living creatures (excluding mosquitoes and assorted blood-suckers). Dr. B, on the other hand, had an unfounded fear of *frogs*. He could never place where the phobia originated but he always assumed it had something to do with his Grandma telling him, "Handling frogs would give a boy warts." Or was it his Grandma who had the warts that she had gotten from handling frogs? Regardless of the reason, Dr. B disliked frogs.

On one occasion, this frog anxiety proved to be a source of considerable discomfort for Dr. B. While the rest of the family was preparing for a trip, young Tyrell had disappeared, as was his usual custom when there was any work to be done. He had gone to play with the frogs in a nearby pool on the Buckenflush farm. Once Dr. B realized Tyrell had skipped out on his chores, the lad was in trouble.

When located, Dr. B proceeded to admonish his son for not being responsible. While his father lectured him, Tyrell stood silently with his hands behind his back. When Dr. B had finished speaking, he turned to walk away. Tyrell seized this opportunity to deposit his newest catch. From behind his back he withdrew a mammoth bullfrog he had named Jaws and deposited it into his father's over-sized shirt! This development would have surprised anyone let alone a person with an irrational aversion to frogs. And when Tyrell hollered, "There's a frog in your shirt!" Dr. B went crazy!

He careened around the yard, fell into a small fishpond, jumped up, fell over the retaining wall and rolled on the ground. Poor Jaws, seeking the quickest way out of "Froggie hell" went with gravity and crawled down into Dr. B's shorts! As Dr. B continued to gyrate and holler, Jaws crawled deeper! During his convulsions, Dr. B fell and landed on his rear end where there was a loud squishing sound! Dr. B quickly pulled off his pants and a bedraggled but still breathing Jaws hopped from the recesses of Dr. B's anatomy.

Tyrell chose this opportunity to disappear for a couple of hours.

What really happened?

We do have a lot of frogs in our ponds. As a child, Ty did find a large bullfrog and named him Jaws. One time we had a visitor who heard Jaws, croaking one evening. She thought it was a moose.

As a child, my son Ty developed a great knack for disappearing when there was work to be done. He usually found more important things to occupy his time.

The rest of this is fabrication; except my Grandma did have warts.

THE EDGE EFFECT

Canoe paddling is a fun activity and usually brings out the kid in most people. The very nature of being outdoors and the freedom to take your canoe where you want is a significant form of self-expression. This combination of freedom and fun provides the perfect setting for relaxation.

For Dr. Odell Buckenflush, the opportunity to relax in a canoe was one of the greatest gifts in life. He viewed the canoe as a perfectly designed craft for boating recreation as well as a great place to "catch 40 winks." He would lay back in the stern seat and rest his shoulder blades across a paddle and be snoring in minutes. In his opinion, the only place better to catch a quick nap was a warm gravel bar next to the river.

One summer the extended Buckenflush family decided to do a family reunion on the Buffalo River in Arkansas. The plan, as contrived by Dr. B, was for the entire clan to do a float trip on the Buffalo River. He provided the canoes and selected a section of river that was about a four hour float. He felt this would allow time for swimming, sunning, picnicking, and, his favorite activity, napping on the river. The weather was perfect and the Buffalo was beautiful. All was right with the world as the Buckenflush armada took off.

Sometimes memorable things happen on a river and this trip had a number of events worth recalling. Lulu Belle managed to delay the trip somewhat when she threw a full metal water bottle to her son, Tyrell. The bottle conked him on the head and sunk in an eight foot section of the Buffalo. Tyrell spent about 20 minutes diving before he got his drink of water. Another incident involved Bezell Buckenflush dropping his only set of eyeglasses in the river. Luckily, Jayrell was able to dive and find the glasses so Bezell did not have to break out his seeing-eye-dog. Willie Joe Wiley, (Odell's Father-in-law) was his normal self. He claimed he never sunburned, only tanned. Of course he ended the day with 2nd

degree sunburn. However, the one event that caused the most hilarity involved Dr. B and his nap time.

The family had pulled up to a nice gravel bar to swim and snack. Dr. B took this opportunity to lie back in his beached canoe and catch 40 winks. He had been paddling with his favorite partner, Lulu Belle. As Dr. B snoozed, Lulu Belle went for a swim. Upon returning to the canoe Dr. B was still asleep. Lulu Belle was toweling off and talking and misjudged exactly where the seat was in the canoe. When she sat down, she missed the seat and sat on the edge of the canoe (the gunnel). The canoe was sitting partway on the gravel bar and partway in the Buffalo River. It immediately tipped over, ejecting Dr. B and Lulu Belle into the river! They both looked like drowned rats as they came to the surface, spitting water and uttering unintelligible sounds. Dr. B did express himself using a couple of terms that were understood though not appreciated by some of the family. At the exact moment Dr. B and Lulu Belle sputtered to the surface, Willie Joe Wiley yelled, "smile," and snapped a picture! That moment proved to be the most remembered and best documented part of the Buckenflush Buffalo River Family Reunion.

What really happened?

This tale was inspired by a few different river events.

One involved my son Ty and my cousin Suzy and it occurred on a Spencer Family Reunion. Ty was about half asleep, lying back in the canoe which was partially on a Buffalo River gravel bar. Suzy had just returned to the canoe taking some dry towels to her brother and sister-in-law who had capsized their canoe and gotten drenched. Suzy was talking and not focusing on what she was doing when she misjudged exactly where the seat was in the canoe and sat on the gunnel, tipping the canoe and ejecting Ty into the river. Ty came up sputtering!

During that same family reunion, one of my sons dove and found the metal water bottle poorly thrown to him by his mother who was under the assumption that it would float.

Our family reunion and float trip on the Buffalo was an enjoyable experience--for some members of the family.

THIS IS KANSAS, DOROTHY

Camping out can be a truly memorable experience. Most of us remember tent camping as youngsters and revel in the stories.

Jayrell and Tyrell Buckenflush definitely enjoyed camping out. They eagerly anticipated the camping experience and took advantage of most every opportunity that came their way. They especially looked forward to the summer paddling and camping trips with their parents Dr. Odell and Lulu Belle Buckenflush. Often, the clan would drive for long distances and not stop until absolutely necessary.

One such trip found them in Western Kansas, heading home from a week of paddling in Montana. When Dr. B became too sleepy to drive further, he pulled the family truck into a roadside camping area and proceeded to set up camp. Dr. B and Lulu Belle set up their tent while Jayrell and Tyrell collaborated on setting up their own tent.

That night, a "Kansas Blow" (very strong wind) came up. When Dr. B climbed out of his tent to check on the boys, he beheld a scene that would frighten any parent. The boys' tent had blown over and was held in place by *only one stake*! Jayrell had fallen out and was sitting outside of the tent with a dazed look on his sleepy face.

At that point the last stake gave way and the tent went rolling across the campground! As the tent rolled away, Tyrell was heard hollering, "I can't get out! I can't get out!" After about 10 rotations, Tyrell fell out of the tent, a little shook up but unharmed. At that point, the wind caught the tent and it sailed across the flat terrain of Kansas never to be seen again.

The remainder of the night was less than restful for the parents as both boys joined them in their small two person tent. The next day the harrowing truth was realized. A tornado had hit 15 miles away, destroying much of the adjacent town. The Buckenflush adventure had been a near disaster.

What really happened?

This tale is based upon a true story. Our family was coming back from a week of paddling in Montana and the boys were indeed ejected from their tent by the wind as described. This event occurred at a roadside campground near Russell, KS, the home of former Senator and past Presidential candidate, Bob Dole. A tornado did touch down in the next community to the west of Russell resulting in considerable damage and destruction. The remains of the boys' tent were found the next day on a fence row about 200 yards away.

CHLORDANE SUCKERS

The following letter was written to the Ozark Daily News, circa 1983, after water quality sampling indicated extremely high concentrations of chlordane in catfish and suckers found in both the James and Finley Rivers in Southern Missouri.

Dear Folks,

In talking with my brother Bezell Buckenflush the other day, he brought up a number of points worth pondering concerning the recent high chlordane findings in fish taken from the James and Finley Rivers. Bezel feels that we have a crisis of enormous proportions on our hands.

Bezel thinks that we *can help* those businesses that continue to sell chlordane as termite control in the area despite the harmful danger chlordane poses to humans. After all, we don't want anyone using harmful chemicals to relinquish their profits. Rather, we want to help these businessmen save money and this can best be accomplished by becoming *their chlordane supplier.*

Since chlordane doesn't break down and there seems to be an overabundance in catfish, carp and suckers (CCS); Bezel thought it wise to remove as many catfish, carp and suckers (CCS) as possible from the James and Finley Rivers and give them, free of charge, to those in the termite extermination business who continue to use chlordane. Those fish (CCS), according to Bezell, could then be used as termite control. The fish (CCS) would simply be placed around the foundations and throughout the many new homes needing termite protection and since there is no new chlordane cost, everybody saves money!

Bezell had some other problems with the James and Finley River chlordane contamination, especially in regards to his favorite spring holiday event, The Nixa Sucker Days. Bezel thought since chlordane doesn't break down, that the people eating suckers at the Nixa Sucker Day festival could also hire out to contractors to just "sit around", thus keeping termites away from whatever they were near.

An added benefit would be the reduction of burial sites as we could eventually just place the bodies of people who have eaten the fish (CCS) under houses. This would provide an additional savings to homeowners by keep termites away and saving on future pest control, not to mention the savings by not having to pay an undertaker for embalming.

Sincerely,
Dr. Odell Buckenflush

What really happened?

As of 2012, the annual Nixa Sucker Days Parade, Festival, and Fish fry has picked up a new sponsor for the event: Cox Health/Hospital in Springfield, MO.

The annual event is now known as Cox Sucker Days.

The above note was posted online at the web address below... and we all know if it is found on the internet, it must be true. http://www.faircitynews.com/2011/05/16/2012-cox-sucker-days-announced/

ODELL BUCKENFLUSH'S
BEST CANOE PURCHASE

Stripper canoes are a beauty to behold. The owners of these boats have not only a good canoe but a crafted work of art. These boats are usually more expensive than other canoes. That coupled with their artistic beauty, means they often end up on display rather than being used like a normal canoe.

Dr. Odell Buckenflush once owned a stripper canoe. It was a 19 foot square stern stripper canoe made from ash and coated in clear fiberglass. It had oar locks, a 5-horsepower engine, and a place to rig a sail if desired. He used the canoe in a variety of ways, fishing, camping, taking Lulu Belle sunning, and even bow-fished out of it.

Dr. B knew this was the most stable canoe he had ever owned and it would be the perfect boat to take his Dad, Buckenflush Sr., on a cruise. Buckenflush Sr. was getting up in years and not partial to any form of canoeing. To make matters worse, Odell had a poor history of keeping his father dry whenever he talked him into going on any type of canoe trip.

Being the canoeing evangelist that he was, Dr. B knew this was a great opportunity for a positive experience. As fate would have it, his father and his father-in-law, Willy Joe Wiley were visiting the same weekend. This was the first time all three were in the same Kentucky location on a beautiful fall weekend.

Putting Willy Joe Wiley and Dr. B together in any adventure usually guaranteed a less than favorable result. As stated previously, Buckenflush Sr. had a terrible canoe history with his son and Dr. B had his own share of solo misfortunate river occurrences. However, Dr. B felt the stars were aligned just right for this trip. After all, even a blind squirrel finds an acorn once in a while!

The Saturday Dr. B convinced his two fathers to go in the stripper canoe proved to be everything the canoe-evangelist thought it would be. For once Buckenflush Sr. had a great time canoeing! Everyone stayed dry and had fun on the best cruise ever on Kentucky's Barren Lake!

What really happened?

Truth is tantamount in this tale. I did purchase a 19' square stern, stripper canoe at a price I could not refuse. It was a beauty and extremely well-made. It had a 5 horse gas engine, could be rigged to sail and had oar locks. I also rigged it with an electric trolling motor and my son and I even Bow-fished out of it.

The only time I ever got my father into a canoe and he stayed dry was the time he and my father-in-law Bill, and I went on a cruise on the Barren Lake in Kentucky. It was Dad's last trip on any kind of earthly boat. He had a great life and passed away after 88 years in January of 2014.

We had a great cruise that beautiful day on the Barren and that trip alone was more than worth the purchase of the canoe. *That trip remains one of my favorite boating memories.*

A VISIT TO THE DARK SIDE

As noted numerous times in previous tales, challenge is relative to the individual. Occasionally, a person with a lifetime spent canoeing will make the move to the Dark Side and commit to becoming a whitewater kayaker. This is a significant challenge and once this commitment is made, the first step of a whitewater kayaker is to develop a bomb-proof kayak roll.

There is a big difference between rolling a canoe and rolling a kayak. Typically, the canoeist works to never have to roll his/her canoe. Because, even if the canoeist is proficient at rolling, after the roll he/she then has to negotiate moving water/rapids with a boat full of water. Developing a roll in a kayak comes easily to some folks and remains difficult for others. In either case, the kayaker must develop a competent roll before attempting to take on whitewater.

Dr. Odell Buckenflush's son, Tyrell had aspirations to become a kayaker. In Dr. B's opinion, he had switched to the Dark Side. While Dr. B. was not necessarily in favor of his son's switch to the kayak, he tried to be a good boater-parent and help his son learn to paddle the kayak. To aid this effort he started paddling a kayak too. After all he was still paddling and a bad day on the river kayaking was still better than a good day at work.

The kayak training continued until Tyrell had his roll down pat. He had successfully completed a combat roll in a local surfing hole and could proficiently roll on either side. **(Note**: A combat roll is a kayak or canoe roll that is performed in a river when one flips unexpectedly). While Tyrell continued to improve as a kayaker, Dr. B's kayak efforts were half-hearted.

The two would occasionally do a roll session together for practice. One time they were working on their kayak rolls in a pool when Dr. B had some trouble completing the roll. When he finally rolled up he had pulled a muscle in his hip!

For the next two weeks, no matter what position he assumed, the pulled gluteus maximus hampered everything in his life. Dr. B tried all sorts of things to get relief from his painful butt, however nothing provided help. After suffering for a couple of weeks of unsuccessful therapy, Dr. B made a decision that proved to be the best course of action: he sold his kayak.

The glass is always half full, right? Dr. B left his temporary visit to the Dark Side and went back to canoeing. He improved his open boating skills and eventually became an Instructor Trainer (IT) in Canoeing with the American Canoe Association. Eventually, Tyrell also saw the light and left the Dark Side. He started paddling whitewater in an open boat. He too became a canoe instructor.

What really happened?

This tale follows closely to the decisions made by my son and myself. Ty went through a phase where he wanted to become a kayaker. At some point he decided to stay with the open boat. This may have had something to do with his outgrowing his kayak. I have not seen too many kayakers that weigh 260 lbs.

During the time Ty was interested in kayaking, I was kayaking too. I was working on my roll when I pulled a muscle in my butt that took forever to heal. To date, it was the worst injury I received while boating. I quit whitewater kayaking, sold my kayak and concentrated on canoeing.

CHAPTER THREE:

Rescues and Survival

NIGHT HIKE

Darkness. Every paddler plans to beat it when beginning a river trip. When the sun goes down, prior to the moon coming up, and you haven't reached the takeout, the river valley can be the darkest place on earth. The last place a paddler wants to be is in the previously described scenario known as "stellar twilight," which is the darkest time of the night. However, almost every veteran paddler has a story to tell about that *one trip* where he or she was forced to walk out.

Dr. Odell Buckenflush has had a number of those unfortunate walks. Paul Pezoldt, the legendary outdoor leadership guru, once noted that some people do not learn from experience unless they are guided in the process. When a young Odell was first told of this statement he replied, "I resemble that remark." Later when Odell became Dr. B, he taught the same concept. However, he expressed it in a less eloquent manner: "Some people are too stupid to learn from experience. They repeat the same mistakes over and over again."

One such walking adventure occurred on a whitewater trip in Tennessee's Obed-Emory Watershed. It was winter and daylight was at a premium when Dr. B, Dead Ted Redd, Jon Nitrus, Jim Grey and Stu Hole decided to venture into the Clear Creek Gorge. They were making the Jett to Nemo run. This was a section most of the group had run previously and while challenging, it was one they could manage.

On this particular December day, the group had gotten a late start. The days are shortest this time of year as it was close to the winter solstice. To complicate matters, the water level was higher than on their previous runs of Clear Creek. Despite all of the negative indicators which should have raised some red flags, they went forward with the trip. They reasoned that the high water would make for a faster run and after all they came to paddle, not turn around and drive home.

Things went fairly quickly on the upper section to Lilly Bridge. However, after this point Clear Creek runs through the gorge section which is extremely remote and difficult to access within the Catoosa Wildlife Management area. From this point on, high water can require numerous scouting stops which may slow a trip considerably. Despite their best efforts, the group made slow progress and visibility worsened with the approach of night. They were a long way from the take-out when the sun went down, accompanied by a moonless night.

Paddling further was out of the question. The companions pulled their boats out and tied up well above the high water mark. They gathered what gear they thought would assist them and set off with a total of two flashlights. After about 30 minutes of use, both flashlights expired. With only the stars to guide them, they were in a real pickle. After scrambling through some undergrowth they were able to make it to higher ground where they saw a light in the distance. Because they had only a vague sense of where they were, they traveled toward the light.

The trip toward the light became a class-IV flood plain scramble through briars, rhododendron, saplings and slick rocks. All the companions had ripped clothing when they took a rest stop and examined themselves. They figured they had ruined one wet suit, two drysuits and all of their footwear was in shambles.

The commute through the woods had taken about two hours. As they got closer to the light, their pace quickened. They were all focused on their destination, oblivious to their suffering from briar scratches, bumps, bruises and the cold. Dr. B was closest to the light and was the first to burst out of the briars into a clearing *back at the river's edge.* About 50 yards away, he could see a campfire shining brightly.

The footing in the clearing was still treacherous and a muddy beaver slide reintroduced Dr. B to the cold water of Clear Creek! His cries of alarm were drowned out by the nearby rapids. Fortunately, the other paddler/hikers came into the clearing from a less hazardous route and were unaware of Dr. B's misfortune.

Unbeknownst to his partners, Dr. B swam the nearby rapid. He washed up on shore on a gravel bar, down river, below the campfire. As soon as he could reach land, he made his way toward the campfire, coming from a different direction.

The campfire was provided by two locals who were coon hunting. The unsuspecting, early season hunters were relaxed and passing a jug between them. Suddenly, four men dressed in dark clothing appeared out of the woods and another came running at them from out of the river. They were surrounded!

At first the coon hunters thought Fish and Wildlife agents were raiding them. As the intruders got closer and their clothing shown in the firelight, they thought it was a Navy Seal team after them. The paddlers' explanations quickly put their fears to rest and the coon hunters encouraged the weary travelers to warm themselves by the fire.

The conversation flowed as the paddlers huddled about the fire for warmth and security. They also were quite thankful for the gracious offering of the sacred jug. Dr. B was still cold from his last river swim and he decided to move closer to the fire for warmth. He positioned himself on the uphill side of the campfire and squatted down. This caused water to squish out of his wetsuit and extinguish the fire!

After Dr. B's fau paux, the coon hunters were glad to get the group of city slickers out of their woods. The paddling group survived that trip a little worse for wear and minus some expensive paddling gear, which was beyond repair. Fortunately, they recovered all of their boats and vowed to get an earlier start next time.

What really happened?

A version of this tale was related to me by my friend, Lee. He and a group of paddlers were paddling Clear Creek in the Obed-Emory system when darkness caught them and forced them to walk out.

The event with the fire being accidentally doused was inspired by events that happened on a winter trip in the same river system. One of our group did the wet-suit-squish, uphill from a fire that we had worked real hard to start. The water from his wet suit put the fire out entirely. Luckily, we found some backpackers with a nice fire about a ¼ mile downstream and warmed ourselves before completing our trip.

HACKY SACK HEAD

When you grow up near a river and live the river culture, you are exposed to a lot of different activities. Every child, spending time near a river will not only swim in the river, but fish, dive into, jump into, run into, and usually swing from a rope into that river. However, the river culture also includes a skilled activity which may be missed in the life of a person not growing up around paddlers. That skilled activity is playing hacky sack on gravel bars.

Playing with a hacky sack (foot bag) was a standard activity among Dr. Odell Buckenflush and his river friends. Riverside hacking on gravel bars is kind of like playing golf in the snow. Much like the poor footing on gravel creates a handicap for playing hacky sack, snow on a golf course would cause obvious problems with footing and visibility. During winter paddling trips one might further handicap themselves by wearing heavy boots while playing hacky sack.

For the uneducated to this sport; hacky sack has some basic standard rules:
1. Participants form a hacky sack circle to play.
2. You never serve the hacky sack to yourself.
3. You cannot touch the hacky sack with hands or arms.
4. Exception: You may serve to another person by tossing the hacky sack with your hands.
5. You may touch the hacky sack with other parts of your body in order to keep it in play.
6. A "hack" happens when all people in the circle touch the hacky sack without it touching the ground. A double hack is when everyone in the circle touches the hackysack twice, without it touching the ground.

Playing hacky sack around a river is an all-inclusive activity, regardless of the age of the participant. As with many other river activities, this game provided the Buckenflush family a way to have fun. Playing in the hacky sack circle always provided exercise and levity. It was also a good activity to warm up prior to a trip, or to kill time while waiting for a shuttle.

On one hacking occasion, Dr. B and friends were on an overnight paddle trip on the Buffalo River in Arkansas. They were hacking on a nice level gravel bar and having a great time. That day, Dr. B was extremely focused and never missed a touch of the hacky sack while keeping it in play. He was "in-the groove". In this "state-of-being", he had a tendency to keep the hacky sack in play using all parts of his body, especially his head. A player in the circle may use their head to hit the hacky sack rather than a foot or knee. As noted previously, Dr. B was playing hard, and was extremely focused and in a state of total concentration. It seemed he could do no wrong and all of his efforts at keeping the hack in play were perfectly timed. This "total state of focus" in any activity has been identified, as "Flow". Considerable research has been performed on Flow and its characteristics.

Flow is what occurs in any activity when the challenge of an activity equals the skill of the participant. If a participant is over-challenged, then the result is anxiety and the participant is not having fun. If the participant is under-challenged, then the result is boredom and the participant is not having fun. So the goal of any activity is to reach "Flow" whereby challenge equals skill, thus keeping the participants engaged in a worthwhile pursuit that they enjoy and is fun for them.

Dr. B was in Flow and it seemed his friends in the circle were too. The hacky sack circle was made up of paddling friends that included Jon Nitrus, Dead Ted Redd, Stu Hole, Hosehead Gray and Jim Gray. They had been hacking on the gravel bar for about 15 minutes but no one was sure of the time because a characteristic of Flow is that participants "in Flow" often lose track of time.

A special note here: Jon Nitrus was a very good hacky sack player. His skill could probably be attributed to his martial arts training, using his feet as defensive/offensive weapons. During this game, he had made repeated saves with high kicks and had lifted the hacky sack where the next player could easily keep it in play. The group was trying for a triple hack and only Dr. B had failed to touch it for a third time. Suddenly, the hacky sack fell toward the center of the circle (no-man's land). Dr. B leaned in to hit the hacky sack with his head. Jon Nitrus also tried to keep the hacky sack in play by wheeling toward the center with a flying crescent-kick. His foot struck Dr. B in the chin as Dr. B's head hit the hacky sack! The concussion of the kick KO'ed Dr. B and split his chin wide open!

After about two unconscious minutes while lying on his back, Dr. B regained consciousness and the first thing he heard was Dead Ted Redd telling him he had completed the triple hack. To which he replied, "What's a hack?" Stu Hole provided first aid to Dr. B in the form of direct pressure to the chin wound using his doo-rag. Some duct tape was unwound from a water bottle and an improvised butterfly stitch was placed on Dr. B's chin to hold the sides of the laceration together.

Dr. B still does not remember much about that particular hacky sack game. He has a nice scar from the Nitrus kick and subsequent duct tape butterfly stitch and he continues to play hacky sack.

What really happened?

This tale was inspired by numerous games of hacky sack. One time I did receive a kick to the face playing hacky sack when I leaned in to "head the sack." The resulting kick to the face split my chin open and definitely *left a mark*.

THE FLOOD OF '93

The Mississippi River flood of 1993 caused considerable hardship for many people in the United States. However, it was another opportunity to paddle for many erstwhile whitewater boaters residing in the Midwest. The massive amount of water also produced whitewater in some very unusual places.

Dr. Odell Buckenflush happened to be in St. Louis when the Mississippi River went over the levee. He took the opportunity to paddle the flooded city streets. As fortune would have it, the current led down a street where strategically abandoned cars had combined to produce a class III rapid. The location of this rapid allowed a paddler to run the rapid, and catch an eddy behind a Walgreen Store. The boater could paddle around the store through an alley, do a quick ferry, attain another eddy and be back above the class III rapid! This allowed Dr. B to repeat the class III run, while never having to get out of his canoe to shuttle.

Dr. B was having a great time paddling but he was getting tired. Above the class III rapid he eddied out behind a stalled car to rest. All at once a guy jumped from the car into Dr. B's canoe! It seems this stranded driver thought Dr. B was coming to rescue him. This was news to the startled Dr. B who accepted his new tandem partner without saying much.

Handing the new partner his spare paddle, Dr. B never missed a stroke as he peeled out of the eddy and again ran the class III rapid. This was a surprising development for the new bow paddler. After catching the Walgreen eddy and heading back toward where the new passenger had first jumped from his car into Dr. B's canoe, the new passenger made a hasty exit *back onto the roof of his stalled car*. As he crawled back into his car, he said, "Thanks, but no thanks, I'll take my chances in the car."

What really happened? This tale is a bunch of hogwash.

THE DARWIN AWARD
FOR CAMPING

NOTE: THE DARWIN AWARDS ARE GIVEN ANNUALLY FOR PEOPLE CAUSING THEIR OWN DEATH DUE TO PERFORMANCE OF STUPID TASKS.

It is human nature to pass on our learning experiences to others. Some folks make a career out of this and become teachers. Others do it instinctively, passing on all sorts of wisdom and experience in any number of varied settings. Regardless of the motivation, throughout history, knowledge has been passed on to subsequent generations albeit not always successfully.

Dr. Odell Buckenflush grew up with a family tradition of camping. His diverse interests in outdoor recreation eventually evolved into a teaching profession that allowed him to pass on his knowledge to others. As an outdoor educator, he had been teaching groups various skills for well over 20 years. During one of his past classes he was on a canoe camping trip teaching Leave-No-Trace and outdoor skills. Unlike other such classes, events unfolded that developed into a significant learning experience for not only the students but the instructor as well.

As with most folks, there are some things that Dr. B figured were just common sense. However, after the occurrence explained below, he decided to re-evaluate that assumption. It was the first night of a 3-day canoe camping trip and the group was in the process of setting up tents in an established camping area. One of the participants came to Dr. B with a problem. The individual had completed setting up the tent and it did not look real taut. There is a learning curve with stake and guy line placement with any tent. This is usually a discovery process and it was Dr. B's practice to not step in too quickly during this process. He figured this person's concern was tent related.

However, the problem brought to Dr. B's attention was not about the tent. Rather, the student complained that their cooking fuel bottle (20 oz. white gas canister) was leaking. Dr. B suggested checking the O-ring or perhaps the lid had gotten cross-threaded. The individual replied, "No, the bottle started leaking after pounding the metal tent stakes into the ground with it." Dr. B was dumbfounded! Even though this was an aluminum canister, the potential for disaster was evident to anyone with a lick of sense.

Put bluntly: fuel + impact + metal = boom!

This person was definitely a candidate for the Camping Darwin Award.

What really happened?

This tale was inspired when a college student of mine did this in an outdoor activities class while camping. Luckily, there was no fire or explosion. I am not sure if the person is still living at this time.

SHUTTLE RUNNER DÉJÀ VU

Paddlers, boaters and fishermen often visit places on rivers that remind them of similar places they have paddled or fished previously. With the many different rivers most boaters and fishers frequent, invariably they have Déjà vu feelings. Or as Yogi Berra, the old New York Yankees manager put it, "It's Déjà vu all over again."

Dr. Odell Buckenflush once had a memorable time on a river that left a strong déjà vu feeling. He had spent a portion of his formative years in Fayetteville, Arkansas, home of the "Whooo, Pig, Soooie, Razorbacks." Throughout this region, his grandfather had served numerous congregations as a Baptist minister. As a grandchild of a preacher and son of a "PK", he often found himself in religious settings. One of those memorable settings was a church camp somewhere in the Ozarks.

Flash forward about 25 years.

Dr. Odell Buckenflush and two friends were on a June boating trip of the Mulberry River, which is a nice whitewater stream south of Fayetteville. The stream was fun and had a number of nice surfing spots where the group played for a very long time. In fact, they took so much time on the river that by the time they reached the take-out, they had missed the agreed upon rendezvous time with their shuttle driver. The aforementioned driver had left an alternate phone number for them to call when they finally got to the take-out. Unfortunately, when they called the phone number there was no answer. It was getting late and they had to make a decision on how to get back to their truck. After a brief discussion, they decided to "hoof it" back to the put-in.

Dr. B drew the "short straw" and began the eight mile trek back to their vehicle. He had been doing a lot of distance running and he viewed this as just another workout that he could run. As is often the case in June in the Ozarks, it was windless and humid. In no time Dr. B was *walking rather than jogging*. He had opted not to carry any water and found himself very thirsty after a full day paddling. All at once he had the strongest Déjà vu feeling he had ever felt.

As he took stock of his surroundings, he realized he was at the entrance to the *same church camp* he had attended as a child! The camp was currently in session and there were a number of campers on the grounds. Feeling like a valued alumnus, he walked into camp and addressed the first person he saw, a young lad of about 8 years and asked where a guy might get a drink. The young boy promptly turned and ran away yelling, "Stranger-Danger! Stranger-Danger!"

Dr. B was mortified! Rather than chase the young child, he froze in place waiting for the inevitable supervisor to show himself. But instead of just one supervisor appearing, three big ol' boys emerged quickly from a nearby building and surrounded Dr. B! While not being a little guy, Dr. B was dwarfed by the huge big ol' boys as they arrived with a "take no prisoners" mentality.

The "fight or flight" reaction occurs in all mammals. It may be manifested in a number of variations other than running away or fighting. One may have loose bladder or bowels, start crying, vomit, get nauseous and even may go into a state of shock (also referred to as whimp-ogenic shock by some). Dr. B felt all of these manifestations but did not give in to any of them. Rather, he maintained bladder control and tried to reason with the big ol' boys who literally had the testosterone oozing from their pores. These camp counselors weren't listening to any of Dr. B's reasoning. In fact, Dr. B was on the verge of getting his ass kicked when an older and obviously more experienced camp director showed up on the scene.

The old camp director listened to Dr. B's explanation about being a former camper, seeing the camp, the déjà vu feeling, and running for his shuttle. All the while, the old director kept looking at Dr. B rather skeptically until Dr. B dropped Grandpa Buckenflush's name. At that point, the camp director said, "So your Brother Buckenflush's grandchild? At this point Dr. B was recognized and was treated like the prodigal son come home. After all, he was a camp alumnus! All was forgiven and Dr. B was even invited to stay for the evening devotional. He begged-off on this offer, however, as his two paddling friends were still waiting for their shuttle-runner at the take-out.

It turned out that the three big ol' boys were part of the offensive line with the University of Arkansas football program and had summer jobs at the church camp. As a further coincidence it also turned out that a brother of the biggest Arkansas lineman/counselor had been a baby sitter for Dr. B's boys during the time he was working toward his doctorate at the University of Arkansas. This nice big ol' boy gave Dr. B a ride to his vehicle at the put-in and he was able to finish the shuttle. Once again, Dr. B had another glass-half-full tale and all was copasetic with the world.

What really happened? This tale has quite a few degrees of truth.

The Déjà vu' experience did occur with me once when we ran a shuttle by the camp on the Mulberry River, but camp was not in session. And my Grandfather was a Baptist minister throughout numerous churches in Northwest Arkansas.

I have run on foot for the shuttle numerous times.

I did have a number of Arkansas Football players baby-sit for my boys at various times while running the athletic dormitory during 1998 and 1999 at the University of Arkansas.

SNAKE SHOCK

Sometimes it just seems to be human nature to "rub salt" into a wound. All people have weaknesses and fears that we would prefer not be noticed or ridiculed. However, it seems our species has an "ornery streak" that will manifest itself with a predilection to magnify the weaknesses or fears of others... just because we can. Some might envision this type behavior as bullying. Everybody knows this antagonizing behavior is something that should not be done, but it happens anyway.

A few years ago, Dr. Odell Buckenflush and friends had halfway unloaded their gear for a night of river camping at a primitive site on Kentucky's Green River in Mammoth Cave National Park. They were scrambling up the slick river bank to their tent sites when suddenly, Dead Ted Redd (DTR) jumped backwards as if he had been shot from a cannon yelling "Holy S--t!" The only explanation he gave when asked what was wrong was to repeat "Holy S--t!" As the group gathered to discover what the problem was, they beheld a large (six feet long and about 14 inches in circumference) timber rattlesnake with a whole bunch of rattles. The group was careful not to encircle the obviously disturbed reptile and took a considerable detour to their campsite.

DTR was still suffering from snake shock at the evening meal when Dr. B's rubber snake made its appearance. Many individuals take a perverse pleasure in frightening companions who display a fear of snakes. While the individual's fear is real, the danger from snakes is often exaggerated. In this instance the danger came not from the snake but from the individual Dr. B chose to scare.

As the group gathered to eat, Dr. B was conveniently sitting next to the DTR. The aforementioned rubber snake was placed under DTR's plate when he was not looking. When he lifted his plate and beheld the snake; he again screamed his favorite slogan in fright! In his fright/flight to escape the snake, he spilled his food all over Dr. B, knocked him down and stepped in the middle of his chest while escaping the reptile. The entire group enjoyed the scene, primarily at the expense of the disheveled Dr. B.

What really happened?

The "holy s—t!" part of the story was the way one of my students reacted to seeing a timber rattlesnake in a similar occurrence. We were camping on the Green River in Mammoth Cave National Park when he nearly put his hand on a really big snake while scrambling up the river bank.

The rubber snake did not appear… on that trip.

And I have been knocked down by a man who stepped right in the middle of my chest as he ran over me. He weighed about 320 pounds and had football cleats on.

CARTOON FALL!

Getting into a canoe that is resting in water can be a rather interesting event. While many canoe access points are nice smooth beaches, there are just as many that are fraught with obstacles. Add some downed trees with a steep, damp river bank and getting into one's canoe may become quite an adventure.

Dr. Odell Buckenflush has had opportunities to enter and exit canoes in all manner of conditions. One time he was on a camping trip with a class on the Big South Fork of the Cumberland River in Tennessee. The banks were pretty steep and to access the shore, the group was forced to utilize downed trees. In effect, the fallen tree served as the access loading dock. This required paddlers to load/unload their canoes while negotiating the slick walk as they made camp that evening.

While loading their gear the next morning, Dr. B knew that particular downed tree would be slippery. The tree had already been used by a number of the group as they loaded their respective canoes. Dr. B was the last to load up because he had been sweeping the camp site to make sure no gear was left behind. When it was his turn to traverse the slick log he was unaware how the morning dew combined with the mud from previous loaders had increased the slipperiness. All at once his feet went out from under him and he was running on air *like a cartoon character*! There was no way he could regain his balance! His feet slipped out from under him and he literally flew into the water of the Big South Fork! He ended up stuck head first in three feet of Big South Fork silt with his feet straight up in the air! The first reaction by the students was shock, until Dr. B came up looking like a mud wrestler and giggling like a fool. At that point the whole group fell into the bottom of their canoes laughing at their crazy, muddy instructor.

What really happened?

This tale was inspired by numerous falls into rivers but particularly the time I tried to cross a large mud puddle on a slick log while hiking. I was accompanying a group of students on the hike when I slipped, ran in place for a moment and then fell into the mud puddle, landing flat on my back with my feet up in the air. My students didn't do anything for a moment. At first they were in shock and then they all fell down laughing.

HOW NOT TO POOP
IN THE WOODS

Summer paddling trips to Canada are a must for every paddler. The water and ephemeral beauty of the Canadian north always provide for a memorable experience. The weather may vary but the fishing is usually great. Black flies and mosquitoes are to be expected but these are small inconveniences when compared to the experiential pay-off.

During a past paddling trip to Canada, Dr. Odell Buckenflush and friends had chosen to paddle Ontario's Spanish River. This proved to be a wonderful whitewater and camping experience. The weather was perfect and there were very few black flies on this trip. However, the ever-present Canadian National Bird (mosquito) caused a few problems.

One of Dr. B's companions was Jim Grey, a veteran paddler. Jim had been to the Canadian backcountry many times and was well aware of the challenges and beauty of the country. Toward the end of the 2-week trip, Jim had taken a walk into the bush because of the urge to purge. After about five minutes a yell was heard and Jim came running out onto a gravel bar, clothes askew and swatting at mosquitoes. In Canadian sign language this means, "Are we having fun yet?"

As he stumbled over toward his wife, he said, "Man, the bugs were so bad back there that I didn't even get to finish wiping! Do I have poop on me?" Of course he did and everyone burst out laughing. From that time on his friends referred to him as: Jim Grey-Poop-on.

What really happened?

A similar event occurred on a Canadian paddling trip with some of our friends. As we remembered it, our friend Shane, ran out of the woods swatting at mosquitoes after a back-country poop and that was when he asked the "Poop-on me question." My friend Ted was on this trip and also wrote a story about this event.

NOGGIN' KNOCKER

River travelers have probably been carrying their own brand of liquid refreshment ever since the first boat trip occurred. A cooler full of the beverage of choice has become standard equipment for many river runners. This tradition has provided many a paddler with considerable gratification, sustenance, and merriment, depending upon the beverage and the state of mind of the boaters.

During a river trip on the Piney River in Arkansas, Dr. Odell Buckenflush and a group of friends were having a very enjoyable float. The water was warm, the cooler was full and the company was great on this ideal Ozark afternoon.

As the group entered a relatively swift rapid known as "1, 2, 3, surprise", Dead Ted Redd requested a can of his favorite beverage from Dr. B, who was carrying the cooler. Dr. B grabbed a can to throw to Dead Ted. Just as Dr. B was about to toss it, his bow partner, Lulu Belle said, "Odell, don't you throw that can!" Dr. B stopped in mid-throw.

The following occurred in a span of about one second:
1. Dead Ted heard Lulu Belle's "order" and saw the interrupted throw.
2. Dead Ted turned his attention to the rapid.
3. Dr. B "thought" about not throwing the can, but then fired a head high bullet at his buddy, whose attention was now elsewhere.

The can struck DTR above the right eyebrow, caromed off his head and landed in the river! Hollering in pain, DTR fell out of his boat and into the river. He said a few choice words, washed into an eddy, salvaged the can, popped the top and was relaxing by the time Dr. B brought him his boat. Dr. B offered excessive apologies for the accurate if not well received throw. DTR's only comment was, "Next trip I'll haul the cooler."

What really happened?

This story was inspired by an event that occurred while I was coaching football at the University of Missouri. We were in a session diagraming plays on a series of playbook forms. Our offensive coordinator told me to "throw him the whiteout" (In those days, whiteout came in a heavy "<u>solid</u>" bottle). I started to throw it, when one of the other coaches said, "Don't throw that." So I hesitated. Then, as John still had his hands up, I went ahead and chucked it head high. It struck him above the right eye and must have hurt like hell. At that point, I was in trouble again; definitely a Buckenflush move.

HOW LOW CAN YOU GO?

Obstacles on a river are a natural part of the landscape. Boaters and fishers get used to negotiating strainers (downed logs and debris), holes (turbulent drops within the current) and severe water temperature changes. However, often the man-made obstacles are more dangerous than any natural ones.

For Dr. Odell Buckenflush, one of the scariest river challenges he ever faced was man-made. He was leading an autumn canoeing class on Drakes Creek in Southern Kentucky. The water in Drakes Creek was pretty low as it had been a dry fall season. Drakes Creek runs through farming country and it was not unusual to encounter a cow or two wading in the creek.

Dr. B was a strong advocate for providing water to cattle via farm ponds. To him, this always seemed the most logical way to water cattle. It is also the best option for maintaining stream bank vegetation and keeping stream water quality in the best possible condition. Fencing cattle in a field also contained cattle while keeping them out of the river. The oft-disputed point was how close the fence should be to a river.

The concept of "we all live downstream" has not always been accepted in parts of Kentucky. Most Kentuckians are very independent and do not like being told what they can and cannot do with their property along rivers and streams. Some cattle farmers continue to graze cattle next to the river without regard for downstream water quality.

On the Drakes Creek trip, Dr. B and his armada of students rounded a bend in an oft-paddled stretch of the river. Something was wrong and it took a minute to realize what was different about this section of river. A wire had been stretched across the river at a height of about 2 feet above the surface! It held the tell-tale signs of being an electric fence with the wire attached to white insulators. It was or had obviously been charged at some point in time.

Dr. B was not real fond of electricity, having had past experiences with electric fences. One of his favorite lines addressed the way we learn and was delivered by Will Rogers:

> *"There are three kinds of (people):*
> *Those that learn by reading.*
> *The few who learn by observation.*
> *The rest of them have to pee on the electric fence for themselves."*

This line seemed appropriately apt at this point in time. What was the trip leader (Dr. B) to do?

How could one determine if the wire was live? He sure wasn't going to "pee on the fence." The only sure way was for someone to touch the wire. As there were no volunteers, Dr. B decided it was his responsibility to be the test dummy. First he got a wooden stick to see if he could lift the wire and allow the other canoes to pass under the wire. This proved satisfactory and in doing so, he did not have to be the test dummy and actually touch the wire.

Canoe after canoe safely negotiated beneath the wire while Dr. B held up the fence. The paddlers hunkered down and passed under without any negative consequence. After the last canoe had passed, Dr. B perceived his personal challenge to negotiate the wire. He had not thought to ask one of his students to hold the wire for him. They had drifted quite a ways downstream and were waiting for him to join them.

He decided to get his canoe as far past the electric wire as he could while still holding the wire up with the wooden stick. He was in a kneeling position and planned to drop the stick and let the mild current drift the canoe downstream while he would *limbo under the wire.* Dr. B lay as far back as he could (limbo style) and it looked like he would clear the wire; except his nose was pretty close. As he began this maneuver he heard one of his student's yell, "How low can you go?"

Just as Dr. B was about to clear the wire, his nose touched the **live** electric wire! He yelled a few choice words from the pain of the shock. Immediately, he heard the same student say, "Apparently, not low enough."

What really happened?

This tale was inspired by a similar occurrence that happen to a class I was teaching a few years back. An electric wire was stretched across the river to keep cattle from leaving the owners property. I received a small shock when I tested the wire.

So nobody else would get shocked, we used a wooden paddle to allow all the canoes to get under the wire. The sweep boat was my son Ty, who has had a bad history with electricity which began when he stuck a paper clip in a wall socket as a child. Ty was clear of the wire but managed to touch it anyway and he got a jolt. To this day I am not sure if he did it on purpose or not.

The land owner was forced to remove the illegal electric wire (it is illegal to fence across a navigable river in KY) and we have had no recurring problems.

CLOSE CALL

One of the most dangerous parts of the paddling experience is actually the travel involved when transporting boats and people during the shuttle. The job of shuttle driver is often perceived as a necessary evil by most boaters and an activity often completed with bored complacency by the shuttle driver.

With Dr. Odell Buckenflush the shuttle was seldom a boring ritual. Something always seemed to occur to liven up his shuttle experience. While running one of his more memorable shuttle trips, Dr. B survived a very close call.

He was pulling a trailer loaded with canoes and kayaks. His route traversed a typical Tennessee Cumberland Plateau road with the standard blind curves, potholes and bumps. Upon entering an infrequent straight section of road, he glanced at his rear-view mirror and observed that a kayak had shifted on his trailer. It was in a dangerous position directly behind the driver's seat and he knew he had to re-tie the kayak as soon as possible. He spied a wide spot on the shoulder of the road and quickly pulled onto it. As he skidded to a stop he jumped out of the truck door.

The sudden stop further loosened the kayak and sent it crashing through the rear window, right where Dr. B had been sitting! Not only did it crash through the rear window of the car, but the momentum propelled it through the front seat also. It would have skewered Dr. B had he stayed seated a split second longer!

What really happened?

I heard of a similar event from my friend Jim about a Tennessee buddy of ours that survived to paddle some more. The car window was shattered when the canoe went in a couple of feet.

TECHNOLOGY CONUNDRUM

How much technology is "too much" on the river? With the continual changes and upgrades of hand-held devices, paddlers can have most all of their electronic needs at any time while on the river. While these electronic needs may be available, it does not necessarily follow that they must or should be used.

During the time when Dr. Odell Buckenflush was residing in Kentucky he and his friends Jon Nitrus and Dead Ted Redd often paddled the rivers of Central and East Tennessee. During one of these paddle trips, the group opted to paddle a section of the Wolf River, near the home of Medal of Honor Winner Sgt. York. The scenic Wolf River runs through Pall Mall, Tennessee. There is a park across from Sgt. York's home which was a standard stopping point for refreshment when paddling the rivers in the area.

After a short breakfast in Pall Mall, Dr. B and his friends chose to paddle a more remote upper section of the Wolf River. The river was serpentine and continually had a number of blind turns. While not requiring scouting of every blind turn, it did cause the group to get spread out. Knowing this section of the river prior to running it, Jon Nitrus had elected to bring his newest toy. He had recently purchased a pair of hand-held CB wireless remote radios. He gave one to Dr. B and kept one for himself. However, he had not anticipated Dr. B keeping up an ongoing broadcast similar to a basketball play-by-play announcer using CB lingo to the extreme. Every few minutes Dr. B launched into a description of his superb paddling ability as he maneuvered the many turns in the river. This obnoxious use of the hand-held CB had about convinced Jon Nitrus to get rid of the radios or at least to keep them turned off in the bottom of his gear bag.

Jon was only half-listening to the hand-held CB when a loud squawk coming from his CB receiver caught his attention. When he responded, "Come back?" Dr. B yelled, "Grab your throwrope; I'm swimming! I'll be washing by any moment!" Dr. B had fallen out of his canoe and was washing downriver while still talking on the CB radio!

Jon quickly pulled to the bank, grabbed his rope and was ready when Dr. washed around the bend and through the small rapid. Jon fired a perfect throw to Dr. B and swung him into an eddy. Dr. B gushed his heartfelt thanks for Jon's quick use of the throwrope. To which Jon replied, "That's a big 10-4, gabby buddy!"

What really happened?

Everyone has opinions of how much, (if any) technology should be employed on river trips. It depends on a lot of different variables.

CHAPTER FOUR:

Philosophy and Life

FLOATERS AND SINKERS

Every person who has ever paddled a river has had the opportunity to drop something into the water at some time. Sometimes that item may be counted as lost once dropped. Some items will float and some will sink. But most of the time we try to retrieve the lost item.

People may sometimes be viewed in a similar way. In life, some people sink and some people float. It is amazing how some people always seem to fall into trouble and come out smelling like roses, while others get stuck in a morass of trouble. Dr. Odell Buckenflush had an old college football coach that phrased it more crudely. He said, "We are all turds in the same toilet. Some of us are floaters and some are sinkers."

In the life of Dr. Odell Buckenflush, trouble tended to follow as closely as his shadow. While he never was a "sinker", he did seem to always be a trouble magnet. The silver lining to this negative tendency was that in spite of all challenges, he always perceived the glass as half-full rather than half-empty. This view toward life developed a lifetime philosophy that produced many a smile and was continually viewed as an opportunity for learning. The opportunity to learn experientially impacted his teaching, inventing and family relationships.

Consider the old saying, "The apple doesn't fall far from the tree." So it has been with Dr. B's children. Both Jayrell and Tyrell have learned experientially from their father's creative adventures and their mother Lulu Belle's Spartan viewpoints. All children go through stages in their life where they get into trouble and learn from the experience. There was a period of time when the Buckenflush boys were viewed like Velcro and Teflon. Jayrell got caught at every little thing he attempted that was not-quite-right. He was Velcro, while Tyrell could do the same not-quite-right thing and not get caught. He was Teflon. Over time these tendencies have switched back and forth. But during this maturation process, each boy has learned experientially.

Experiential learning has been integral to the Buckenflush family maxim: <u>Learn from your mistakes and do not repeat the same mistake</u>. Otherwise that would be the standard definition of *insanity* which is, "Doing the same thing over and over while expecting different results."

The Buckenflush view: Continue to persevere, run the good race, never give up, keep your chin up, for the glass is half-full rather than half-empty.

What really happened?

Teflon and Velcro. That is how my wife and I have looked at our boys in numerous situations. And my wife is definitely a very low-maintenance Spartan.

BRUTE FORCE WILL GET
YOU NOWHERE

Working with at-risk youth in outdoor, experiential learning settings can be very rewarding. The setting breaks down barriers with kids and the challenges force them to engage in teamwork. The model has been utilized effectively in many instances as a method to reach kids that do not quite fit in a traditional education system.

A few years ago, Dr. Odell Buckenflush and his friend Dr. Joe Giant took an adventurous float trip with a group of at-risk high school students. The hot July paddling route was the Wild and Scenic Jacks Fork River in Southern Missouri. This group of students was extremely active and ornery. They included a number of kids who were classic examples of the descriptive diagnosis: Attention Deficit Hyperactivity Disorder (ADHD).

Dr. B was hired as the trip leader and canoe instructor. He had planned to give some basic paddle instruction prior to floating the river but it quickly became obvious he needed to change plans due to the short attention span of his students. The canoe instruction session was not going to be successful unless he quickly began *active* paddle instruction.

He had begun the instruction session in an icy cold spring-fed tributary of the Jacks Fork. Two particular ornery teenage students continued to disrupt the class making instruction quite difficult. Dr. B decided it was time to help the boys "focus" with a little cold-water discipline. He drifted next to the two disruptive boys and had them in his sights, all the while continuing his instruction. He wound up to demonstrate a low brace paddle stroke; intending to soak the two ornery boys with cold water. When Dr. B hit the water with his paddle, the force of the blow snapped his paddle in half! With surprise on his face, he slowly rolled over into the icy waters of the spring for he had no paddle with which to brace.

The entire class "whooped it up" at Dr. B's expense. They thought the frigid roll and swim the best part of the instruction. In spite of the active nature of the students, they had a lot of fun and eventually became thoroughly engaged in canoeing.

"**Brute Force Gets You Nowhere**" but it can provide entertainment.

What really happened?

This tale was inspired by a real and very good trip that resulted in some interesting occurrences that appear in other tales. The trip was on the Jacks Fork and was set up by my buddy Joe. I did break my paddle and slowly rolled over in the coldest spring-fed river in Missouri and from that point on have used the paddling instruction maxim: "**Brute Force Gets You Nowhere.**" It is now on a sign in my classroom.

One of our co-instructors, Brandon, made the following comment about one of the at-risk youth on the trip. The student was explaining how he could skateboard off the top of our post-trip dinner building which would carry him to an adjacent building and then to another rooftop. Brandon succinctly summed up what he thought was the kid's projected future: "Dead by 18."

ONE TOUGH TOWN

The Missouri River has been eloquently described in the expedition journals of Meriwether Lewis & William Clark. The upstream and overland segments of their journey required a yeoman's effort by all members of the expedition. They had to be mentally and physically tough people to complete the 16-month expedition. This toughness seems prevalent in folks who have elected to live in the shadow of the Lewis & Clark's expedition along the Missouri River in Montana.

On a past canoeing trip in Montana, Dr. Odell Buckenflush paddled the easy direction on the Missouri River (downstream). However, on Dr. B's trip down the Missouri, the thing he remembered most vividly occurred in a town that had a reputation throughout its history as "one tough town".

Fort Benton, Montana, was first an old trading fort then evolved into a river town. It served as the jumping off place for the Bozeman Trail and was as far as folks went on the Missouri River before they headed overland toward Oregon or the Montana gold fields. During its hey-day, it was often lawless and filled with brothels, saloons and gaming houses. However, that was many years ago. On the summer day when Dr. B reached Fort Benton he had completed about 200 Missouri River miles of his trip. He figured Fort Benton would be just another sleepy river town.

He tied up his canoe and crawled up the steep Fort Benton riverbank next to the downtown park along Main Street. The first resident he noticed was wrestling with something. Upon closer examination, he couldn't believe his eyes! It was a rattlesnake that had to be at least five feet long and its opponent was but a child of 10 or 11 years of age! The boy had the snake in a death grip or vice versa! The snake was wrapped around the boy and rattlin' for all it was worth! Dr. B started to help the child when he was abruptly stopped by an old man of about 75 years who came out of nowhere, grabbed his arm and said, "Whoa there stranger. Let the boy be. If'n he can't handle that snake, then he won't 'make it' here." Dr. B was frozen in fascination as first the snake seemed to have the child and then the boy got the upper hand. While this whole scenario was unfolding, a lady sitting on a nearby park bench was casually reading from a *Reader's Digest*. Dr. B realized that she knew what was going on yet she showed little concern. Finally, the lad was able to grab a stone and dispatch the rattlesnake. The *Reader's Digest* lady indicated satisfaction by nodding her head in approval, smiling and letting out a loud belch. The old man clicked his heels and cackled while the boy pulled out a knife and began to skin the snake.

At this point, had it not been for the *Reader's Digest,* Dr. B thought he had surely walked into a time warp. As he turned around, kind of in a daze, he read a Historical Marker commemorating the town. It read, "Fort Benton, a town with hair on it."

What really happened?

I observed a very similar event in Fort Benton on a solo trip down the Missouri river a few years ago. Upon arriving in the town, there were two kids playing with a large rattlesnake and a lady nearby casually reading a *Readers Digest* and observing the action. Eventually, the two young boys dispatched the snake after playing with it for a while. The slogan on the Fort Benton, Montana sign is verbatim.

ROBBED!

As paddlers become more experienced and their paddling skill improves, they often attend seminars or conferences to learn more. Such is the natural learning progression of many disciplines. For many paddlers the learning and preparation phase takes on an important significance.

Dr. Odell Buckenflush had taken play and learning to a pretty high level. His primary employer hired him to teach university courses in outdoor venues which fit the description of him by his mother-in-law as "The Doctor of Play." Dr. B felt that paddling and learning went together like peanut butter and jelly. He perceived education as a lifelong endeavor and often attended conferences, seminars, and clinics. By adding paddling as a variable to the clinic formula, he could combine play and learning by justifiably attending paddling conferences.

The largest US Conference that ties paddlesport and learning together is the annual American Canoe Association (ACA) conference. At this conference, paddlers of all stripes come together and enjoy seminars, teaching updates, gear swaps, networking and lying. A few years back, the annual ACA clinic was held in Louisville, KY. It was at this conference that Dr. suffered a significant loss.

While he was checking into the hotel hosting the ACA conference, his paddling gear bag was stolen from his Jeep. He was scheduled to teach an instructor course as part of the conference and now he was without the requisite equipment. At least the thief had left Dr. B's paddle in the Jeep.

Initially Dr. B was in shock and very upset with the loss of his gear. However, after a little thought, he reacted as he always does; he viewed this as the glass being half full not half empty. After all, he could borrow gear for the instructor update class at the conference. Being relatively queer-for-gear, this was a great opportunity for him to buy <u>new gear</u>! Even his wife, Lulu Belle, had to agree it was a needed purchase.

What really happened?

True story that happened to me. Yes, I got my gear stolen at the annual ACA conference in Louisville. I had to borrow gear for the instructor class. The glass is always half full and not half empty and I was able to purchase new gear!

My doctorate is in education and recreation and my mother-in-law does refer to me as "The Doctor of Play."

BORDER CROSSING

The border crossing into Canada requires the visitor to have all their "ducks in in a row" prior to entering. It is usually a pretty straight-forward process but can be problematic due to greater restrictions and expectations as one enters Canada. The days of crossing into Canada without proper identification (Passport) are long gone.

During a past river adventure, it was necessary for Dr. Odell Buckenflush and friends to cross the Canadian Border to paddle in Quetico Provincial Park. This was Dr. B's first venture into Canada and his veteran companions were explaining the protocol for the border crossing. They were on a tight schedule and definitely didn't want to go through any lengthy inspection. Knowing Dr. B's love for talking, the trip leader's last bit of sage advice was: "Whatever you do Odell, don't say anything about drugs or guns."

At the customs check, Dr. B began a casual conversation with the customs officer, much to the discomposure of his friends. The conversation was polite and nothing of any significance was discussed and the border guard waved them through. Just as they were pulling out, Dr. B said, "By the way, do you guys really have a lot of trouble with people trying to take handguns into Canada?" The guard replied, "Please pull over to the parking area on your left. We need to examine your vehicle and belongings."

On the return trip across the border, his friends placed a gag over Dr. B's mouth.

What really happened?

This tale was inspired by events that did not quite happen as described, but our trip leader Dave was very serious in making sure we did not say anything that sent up red flags.

THUMPER

Take-out areas for boaters range from the most pristine wilderness settings to highly developed ramps constructed by government agencies. What constitutes a good river access is somewhat relative to the boater. However, all paddlers appreciate an easy access. Some river access sites have camping available adjacent to the access and have become quite popular with paddlers.

One day, Dr. Odell Buckenflush and friends had finished a good day of paddling and were in the process of loading their boats. The group had chosen to take out at a U.S. Forest Service campground where they planned to stay the night. The campground and river access were very popular and provided a number of amenities for the users.

As the paddlers finished loading their boats, a Jeep with the top down sped through the campground, fishtailing and doing about 35 mph over the posted limit! The driver was an obvious hazard to all in the area. Dr. B and others at the access hollered for him to "slow down". However, the driver ignored the angry cries, flashed a well-known hand sign and sped away in a cloud of dust and gravel.

Now the camaraderie of folks on the river is usually in evidence at a take-out area. The boaters have all shared something each can appreciate. This bonding brings people together and in this particular instance, the folks at the take-out reacted as an angry mob. They were outraged! This outsider had violated the sanctity of their holy space!

Unknown to the reckless driver, he was on a one-way campground loop that circled and exited only a few yards from the access and the angry paddlers. Dr. B and his companions knew the area. Though they were still coughing from the dust thrown up by the speed demon, they grabbed their paddles and lined up on either side of the road and waited for the vehicle to "run the gauntlet" at the exit.

When the driver beheld the lineup of angry paddlers, he tried to avoid the confrontation by cutting through an adjacent campsite. Dr. B was closest to the alternate route. As the vehicle sped by, Dr. B reached into the open Jeep and thumped the driver on the head with his paddle! The driver hit his brakes and was about to get out of his vehicle and confront Dr. B when he beheld 10 or 12 angry, paddle-bearing folks running toward him. He decided to beat a hasty retreat and again sped away, throwing gravel in his wake and using his favorite hand sign.

High five's were given all around because Dr. B had avenged the besmirched honor of the river access with his *best stroke of the day.*

What really happened?

The inspiration of this tale comes from my father-in-law, Bill who lives on a street that ends in a cul-de-sac. There is only one way in and one way out of the street. Periodically, cars would speed down the street and neighbors would call Bill on the phone and warn him about the speeding car. Then Bill would wait for the speeder on the return drive from the cul-de-sac. Bill is a pretty big guy and not one someone wants to tangle with. One time when a speeder was driving a convertible, Bill stood by the side of the road with a stick in his hand. As the driver sped by, my father-in-law thumped him on his head and told him to "slow down." That convertible never stopped or came down the road again.

SABBATICAL RESEARCH

College research projects that involve human subjects require the investigator to complete quite a few steps prior to ever gathering any data. The process is quite involved and a number of steps exist to protect the subjects, the college and the researchers. A number of standardized protocols exist for those involved in research and sometimes projects never "get off the ground" due to the bureaucratic process.

Dr. Odell Buckenflush had completed a number of recent research projects following a strand of research that related to "things that happen in outdoor settings". The following statement went out in an attempt to recruit subjects for his proposed research sabbatical:

> This research project targets all people who consider themselves outdoor types but are concerned with necessary bodily functions that must happen in outdoor settings. This research examines: Whether to use the outhouse/ port-a-john/pot/dunny/privy/head/san-o-let toilet or cathole in the woods. After all, pooping in the woods is an art and often a traumatic one at that. The nature of dropping your pants and exposing yourself to nature and all of its minions can be intimidating.

> In an effort to further academia's understanding of this "oh so natural event" I, Dr. Odell Buckenflush am happy to announce a national research project entitled: Cat-holing techniques: The disposition of fecal matter in outdoor settings beneath disturbed earth. My university employer recognizes me as a full professor in the field of outdoor education/recreation. In my mind, that translates into *"expert" in the field of scat disposition.*

The continual aggregation of folks in outdoor settings provides an excellent opportunity for all citizens to make a contribution to the "field of human waste disposition in outdoor settings". These outdoor folks are literally "full of crap" and provide an excellent sample for study. This research project will further increase our understanding of human impacts and builds upon past field research from my two most recent research projects: "Stressful Sphincter Manipulation in Challenging Outdoor Settings" and "Where Porcelain is Scarce".

Pursuant to this research project, I am seeking volunteers for my study which I plan to complete during my upcoming proposed sabbatical. After all, if a fellow faculty member can get a sabbatical to write about "Experience Sampling Methodology to Examine Psychological Profiles of Deer Hunters Involving Mood States and Leisure Antecedents while Deer Hunting in the Woods of Northwest Arkansas," then I am sure my upcoming fecal research will place me in a preeminent place in the honorary fraternity, Phi-Beta-Crappa. Additionally, this research project should bring our esteemed university considerable exposure, thus justifying my sabbatical.

Auditions for research subjects will begin soon. Subjects are encouraged to practice in their backyards prior to auditioning. This should enable subjects to make an adequate estimate of the amount of earth to be displaced prior to defecation. (A small shovel makes a suitable tool for backyard practice). Dates for upcoming auditions will be posted on privies throughout United States Forest Service (USFS), United States Army Corp of Engineers (USACE), National Park Service (NPS) and Tennessee Valley Authority (TVA) recreation areas.

Subjects partaking in this research project will receive rewards in the form of a complementary poop scoop upon completion of defecation. Subjects partaking in this research project, but unable to consummate defecation, will be given laxative candy bars.

If you have read this far, then you most likely are not offended by natural bodily functions; otherwise I suggest you refuse to read further.

Sincerely,
Odell Buckenflush, Ed. D.
Professor of Scat Disposition

What really happened?

My Doctoral Dissertation topic is hidden in this tale.
This document was inspired by a sabbatical I received in 2014, not for studying scat disposition, but rather to write about some.

IMPROVISE AND ADJUST

Boat repairs and duct tape go hand in hand. Any paddler who has had the misfortune to spring a leak, crack a boat hull or mend a broken paddle will swear by the miracle stuff. The ability to improvise and adjust by making field repairs with duct tape have salvaged many a paddling trip and enabled the trip to continue.

One such trip involved Dr. Odell Buckenflush with his paddling buddies Jon Nitrus and Dead Ted Redd. They were paddling the Chattooga River in Georgia. The river was running low and the boats were dragging in the shallow areas. When they reached Dick's Ledge, disaster was close at hand. Dr. B ran the 7-foot drop last and missed his line. He got hung up at the lip of the fall and teetered for an eternally long moment before he dropped over the falls landing upside down! Luckily, he was unhurt but the impact of the drop boke both of the thwarts in his old solo canoe!

After his rescue by his paddling companions, Dr. B and company gathered on a gravel bar below the drop to access their predicament. They were examining the damaged boat and discussing their options when Dead Ted Redd hollered, "Look what I found!" Excitedly, he ran to his friends waving an unbroken used thwart he had found on the gravel bar!

The paddling buddies went to work and in minutes had installed the new-to-them thwart through the magic of duct tape. The second thwart was repaired when Dr. B cut a small sycamore tree limb with his Swiss army knife and duct-taped it to the other broken thwart. The old canoe paddled perfectly for the remainder of the trip. In fact, the repair job worked so well that Dr. B paddled the same boat for another six months before he made permanent repairs.

What really happened?

This tale was based upon true events. My friend Jon dropped over Dick's ledge on the Chattooga, landed upside down and broke both thwarts in his Perception HD (hard-to-stay-dry) whitewater canoe. We found an unbroken thwart on the beach below the falls and also cut a sycamore limb and used duct tape to attach the new thwarts. Jon paddled his repaired boat for a long time afterwards. In fact, I do not know if he ever properly repaired the canoe.

As I recall, that same trip had another boater get hung on the lip of a long drop which resulted in another swim. It was me and not Jon that got hung on the lip of Bull Sluice before dropping over for another Spencer swim.

THE GLASS RUNNETH OVER

When going on a canoeing expedition, travel is a normal part of the experience. The nature of an expedition usually requires travelling long distances that can be quite taxing. Once one makes the commitment to travel, then the travelers' attitude can determine whether it is an enjoyable trip or not. Yes, this could be interpreted as another (glass half full or half empty) story.

It was late summer in Jasper, Arkansas, when the Buckenflush family and friends began their expedition to the Boundary Waters of Minnesota. The group was caravanning and Hosehead Grey was setting the pace, accompanied by Jim Grey, Auburn Redd and Ted Redd, while Dr. B drove the Buckenflush family in his old Isuzu Trooper. In a caravan, it is normal procedure to stay close together and on this expedition the two vehicles were in communication via CB radios. However, because Lulu Belle wanted to see or visit numerous places on the route, the two vehicles often found themselves miles apart, stopping at different times. They continually got separated and even camped at different locations during the two-day drive.

It is interesting how folks in the two vehicles viewed this trip differently. For Lulu Belle, the trip to and from was every bit as enjoyable as the Boundary Waters destination. She fit the old cultural outlook which says, "A truly happy person is one who can enjoy the scenery on a detour." She enjoyed all aspects of travel and her positive attitude usually influenced those who travelled with her (glass half full). However, Hosehead Grey was in a constant state of irritation that they would even consider altering the route to their planned destination. For her, travel to the destination and travel home from a place was a "necessary evil" (glass half empty).

This philosophic difference was never more evident than the return trip to Arkansas. Due to construction, different route choices and some semi-truck accidents, the Buckenflush vehicle ended up about three hours *ahead* of the Grey Vehicle by the time they reached Kansas City. This coincidental occurrence was no big deal to the Buckenflush family. They were in no hurry and would probably stop at least two more times prior to reaching Jasper.

Not so with the Grey vehicle. Hosehead was "fit to be tied." The thought that the Buckenflush vehicle might arrive home prior to her was unacceptable. She refused to let anyone else drive and once the road was clear of construction, she sped homeward. Just past Kansas City she declared, "I'm not stopping again until we reach Jasper." It seemed her bladder was extremely large, which was not the case with her three travel companions. Most folks can relate to this uncomfortable scenario, especially if stuck in traffic after drinking a large beverage.

Hosehead considered the inability to control ones bladder a "personal problem". In spite of the continual begging to stop by her travel companions, Hosehead kept driving. All of her passengers were forced to use any available containers to "relieve themselves" in the car. Dead Ted Redd filled two coke bottles and was in the process of filling his Nalgene water bottle. It was near the top and he was pleading for Hosehead to stop. At this point they all began laughing at DTR's predicament. Eventually, human physiology prevailed and they *all* paid the price for laughing!

Hosehead's vehicle finally overtook the Buckenflush clan near Branson, Missouri. But as they passed, it was noticed that all of the car windows were down. It seems the smell necessitated this action because the "glass was neither half empty nor half full. Rather, *the glass was overflowing!*"

What really happened?

Thanks for the inspiration of this tale from one of my mentors, Bill O'Neill, who was my academic advisor in college, my position coach while playing football in college, and also my boss through some great years coaching. He told a similar story about taking a spring-break trip with friends from Chicago to Florida. He drove and refused to stop so his travelers filled every available container while in route. I have never seen him laugh as hard as when he told this tale.

The characteristics of Lulu Belle Buckenflush while travelling are quite similar to my wife Deb. It is not unusual to drive way out of our way to visit some site on a trip. One time we crossed two state lines off of our intended route so we could visit the Idaho Potato Museum, which advertised, "Free taters for out-of-staters". In her view, the journey is always more important than the destination.

TAKE THE NEXT TURN, RIGHT?

The Yellowstone River is a classic river that should be on every paddler's bucket list. Most trips begin in Gardiner Montana below Yellowstone National Park and consist of some mild white water. The area above Gardiner is within the boundaries of Yellowstone National Park and until recent management policy changes were enacted, could not be paddled legally. However, the thing that makes this such a great river is that it is classified as a Blue Ribbon River renowned for its *trout fishing.*

During a past river trip, Dr. Odell Buckenflush and company had designed a whitewater and fly-fishing extravaganza. They planned to paddle the Yellowstone River from the National Park boundary at Gardiner, Montana, to Big Timber, Montana. The adventure evolved into a guys-only trip when their wives realized fishing was the primary goal.

Upon arrival in Gardiner, Montana, Dr. B and Stu Hole volunteered to drive their vehicles on the 3-hour shuttle. As the shuttle drivers reached the community of Big Timber, Dr. B suggested to Stu (over the CB radio) that they ask a local for directions to their desired take out. With that decided, all that was left was to choose a reliable river source of information.

As they pulled into a general store for gas, a Volkswagen bus with a Blue Hole, OCA canoe and Montana license plates pulled in behind them. Seizing on this fortunate opportunity, Dr. B inquired on the location of the Big Timber access where they planned to leave a vehicle at the take out. The aging local canoeist responded, **"Take the next turn, right. Drive about one mile and you'll hear the sound of the water. That's your take out."**

Dr. B half listened to the somewhat cryptic directions and assumed Stu knew where they should go. Meanwhile, Stu had heard the same message and assumed Dr. B knew exactly where the take out was. This was a normal occurrence for Stu and Dr. B. During past river trips, they had managed to change half-day floats into marathons by the assumption that the "other guy" knew where the take out was.

With the directions to the take out "clearly understood", the drivers proceeded to the take out where they would drop off the van. The "turn in the road" was easy to find and the "sound of water" seemingly was close by on the right. They drove down a twisting road to the take out. Stu noted that the river seemed somewhat small to be the Yellowstone. However, Dr. B said this had to be the place.

They parked the van and drove the truck back to Gardiner to begin the trip. The five days on the Yellowstone were beautiful and the group all agreed it had been a great trip as they pulled into the community of Big Timber.

It was at this point in time that both Dr. B and Stu perceived they might have a problem. The river looked considerably wider near Big Timber than where they had left the van. Additionally, the take out was on the wrong side of the river. Had they missed a bridge crossing that would have placed their vehicle on the opposite side? According to the topographical map, they were at their take out. They could not see their vehicle so they decided to stop and hike into town to check things out.

Upon reaching a nearby ranch, the boys learned they had left their van on the *Boulder River,* which empties into the Yellowstone River just below town! Now they faced a 7 to 8 mile upstream paddle to reach their van. After a brief and one-sided discussion, it was determined that Dr. B and Stu Hole would have the singular honor of the upstream paddle to reach the van while the remainder of the group retired to a nearby gravel bar to await their return.

While fighting the upstream current, Dr. B mumbled that the directions had been to "turn right". Finally, the exhausted paddlers reached *their* take out. They loaded their canoe and gear on the van and headed back to pick up their friends. As they rounded a bend in the road they saw the same Volkswagen bus with the Bluehole OCA canoe on top. It was their local information source, the aging canoeist!

The boys stopped to query the gentleman to determine where they had gone wrong. As he repeated the directions, the blinding light of the obvious shined upon them and the cryptic meaning was revealed: **"Take the next turn... right (<u>understand</u>)? Drive about one mile and you'll hear the sound of the water. (<u>Everybody with any sense knows the Yellowstone is on the left</u>). That's your take out."**

What really happened?

This story was inspired by a fishing trip on the Yellowstone River that occurred in a time prior to use of the now-common GPS systems. Our trip actually had no mix-up on the shuttle. However, most all paddlers can relate to "locals-giving-directions" for river access.

BORDER CROSSING...
REVISITED

Crossing the border into Canada is not always the easiest procedure. Due to greater restrictions and expectations as one enters Canada, all the "I's must be dotted and the T's crossed." The days of crossing into Canada without a passport are long gone.

Dr. Odell Buckenflush had a history of trouble at Canadian border crossings. His troubles always resulted from his inability to keep his mouth shut. It seemed he had a great knack for saying exactly the wrong thing at the worst point in time during the crossing.

Dr. B and friends were again crossing into Canada via the customs station at Sault St. Marie. The group was travelling in three vehicles and they were in communication with each other via CB radios. A general discussion of the upcoming crossing had been in progress and Dr. B had been cautioned (as usual) not to say anything that would cause problems like the last time they crossed into Canada.

As the group pulled up to the crossing, Dr. B noted over the CB how the Canadian crossing attendants looked pretty serious and didn't seem to have much of a sense of humor. The passengers in all three vehicles simultaneously responded, "Shut-up Odell!"

The first vehicle, driven by Dead Ted Redd, passed through without incident. Dr. B was in the second vehicle and he kept his mouth shut and also passed through without any problem. Just as the third vehicle pulled into the customs booth, a loud voice blared over the CB, obviously that of Dr. B, "Hey Ted, I guess you got through customs without them finding your guns and drugs, huh?" Dr. B had forgotten about the third vehicle and their CB radio, which everyone nearby overheard.

The sirens blared and all three vehicles were pulled over to undergo a thorough inspection. Dr. B attempted to explain he was just joking as all three vehicles were emptied and completely searched to the displeasure of six very irate Americans and one mortified Dr. B. As they pulled away after a 2-hour delay, Dr. B said over the CB radio, "I told you those Canadian Border Guards didn't have much of a sense of humor." To this comment came the synchronized reply, "Shut-up Odell!"

What really happened?

Crossing the Canadian border is not a time to make jokes. It is kind of like seeing your friend Jack as you board an airplane. Sometimes you just don't say, "Hi, Jack."

YOU CAN'T DEFEAT
THE RIVER

Throughout life we are challenged to perform. This challenge is often rewarded with trophies for accomplishment, merit or through financial gain. When paddling rivers, the challenge of navigating the river successfully may be its own reward or it may be recognized through the aforementioned methods of reward. Successful navigation of the river may result in the paddler boasting that they have "conquered the river."

So it was during the maturation process of Dr. Odell Buckenflush. During his early years, he looked at rivers as challenges to overcome and be conquered. He was always rather stubborn and had to be shown that rivers are often not what they seem. Experience is a great teacher when paddling whitewater and for Dr. B, the river provided an early lesson in humility, which made quite an impression on him.

Dr. B and friends were paddling the Piney River in Arkansas. The current was relatively swift and Dr. B decided to paddle a different line from that chosen by his more experienced companions. Prior to the choice, a brash Dr. B had proclaimed he could "beat the river", and would be taking the more challenging routes. As could be expected, mishaps occurred. First, he broached on a tree and it took him some time to be extricated from the lone tree on which he had gotten hung. He was razzed considerably for choosing the "best route" in his conquest of the river.

The next day, they paddled the same part of the Piney again. When the group reached the area where Dr. B had broached the day before, he was heard to say, "I'll show this old river it can't beat me." His friends repeated these same words to a humbled Dr. B as they again helped him unpin his broached canoe from the <u>same tree</u>. In honor of continued stubbornness, his friends dubbed the tree, "Buckenflush Willow." And so it is known to this day.

Dr. B is still stubborn, however, he has matured and knows that one doesn't defeat or conquer any river. Rather, one respects, lives and works with rivers. Those who take our rivers and streams for granted or view them as things to be conquered are setting themselves up for failure because when least expected, the river will reach up and grab the proud and foolish boater.

What really happened?

This story was inspired by events that occurred early in my paddling career. I got hung on the same small tree on back-to-back days in a no-name rapid on the Piney River in Arkansas. I was verbally abused by the rest of the paddling party and I have continually been reminded of the event to this day.

EPILOG:

The Doing

During the paddling maturation process, many boaters go through a phase where the river is viewed as an opponent to be beaten. Winning this self-determined challenge may occur when one navigates a river without tipping over or measured by merely surviving when they do tip over. The paddler may then develop delusions of grandeur stating he or she has *conquered* the river.

Outfitters have perpetuated this image with every commercial operation offering shirts for sale proclaiming success on some river. Paddling consumers gladly purchase these mementos of their accomplishments. This concept of having evidence of accomplishment is nothing new. In the 1930's, Aldo Leopold, noted in *A Sand County Almanac*, "Outdoor users seem to consume their recreation pursuits in the most rudimentary forms." Even bird watchers have a basic need to "have evidence" of some accomplishment when checking off an identified species.

When one views The Doing, *purely for the experience of the moment*, then one may better appreciate the river experience. At this point the need to have evidence of accomplishment such as a shirt proclaiming where one has been, or a rock from the area, or pictures taken while running a rapid all become secondary. This concept may be somewhat offensive to some who make a living off paddling tourists. But, sometimes The Doing is its own reward.

For Dr. Odell Buckenflush, <u>The Doing</u> keeps him coming back for more.

THE ODELL BUCKENFLUSH
GLOSSARY OF
RIVER TERMS

This glossary has been included to assist those who are unfamiliar with paddling and other wilderness terms. There are two parts to the glossary: the official definition and a completely fictional entry. _You decide which is which._

ABS -- A type of layered plastic and foam used in the manufacture of canoes, which is extremely durable. Mass-produced as Royalex®. Or Acrylonitrile butadiene styrene—yes, go ahead and try to pronounce it and you'll see why we call it ABS.

ACA -- **American Canoe Association** or **American Camping Association**-- Two groups which continually train instructors for outdoor related activities. Not related, just confusing.

Air Bags -- Inflatable plastic or nylon bags that are placed in a white water canoe to displace water. Or to displace unwanted passengers. These evolved from inner tubes and Styrofoam blocks.

Aft -- A nautical term used to describe an area in a boat behind another place. Or ¾ of a crazy person (Daft).

Amidship -- The center of a boat from end to end. Or where you strategically place the fattest passenger.

Asymmetrical Hull -- A hull shape, not equal (symmetrical). Or two different halves of a canoe/kayak that were mixed up in production and attached together anyway.

AWA -- American Whitewater Association – An association for whitewater boaters. Or a place often considered out of reach as in "Far awa."

Back Band (Back Rest) -- Provides support for the lower back while kayaking and helps with erect posture in the boat. Located behind the paddler. Or the guys in the back of the shuttle vehicle that constantly sing along with the radio.

Bailer -- River trash converted to gear used to bail water out of a canoe/raft. Or the liaison between you and the local sheriff. Or a *get out of jail free* card.

Bang Plate (Skid Plate) -- A protective plate rounding the end of a canoe that is attached or overlaid for protection against impact. Modern versions are commonly made of Kevlar. Or what hungry paddlers do when the food is slow in coming.

Bankers -- A derogatory term used to describe paddlers that cannot paddle a straight line (inability to follow a line or track their boats). On a river they paddle from bank to bank. Or people that most paddlers owe money too…in order to fund their obsession.

Belaying -- The act of providing anchored support to a rope by partially wrapping it around an object (tree or body). Or the art of tanning on a gravel bar as: "I belaying in the sun."

Bent-Shaft Paddle -- A flat-water, racing paddle designed with a slight bend at the throat. Or what happens to a paddle when someone falls on it.

Blade -- The portion of the paddle that is wide and flat and is used to create power. Or the piece of equipment, attached to paddlers' lifejacket (PFD) that allows them to spread peanut butter.

Blue hole -- An area on a river where a spring enters, producing a bluish cast to the water. Or a pretty good canoe.

Boat-Over-Boat Rescue (Canoe-over-Canoe Rescue) -- A rescue maneuver where a capsized boat is pulled over an upright boat and drained. It is then positioned parallel to the upright boat so the swimmers can re-enter. Not a CPR technique.

Booties -- A type of neoprene shoe/boot combination which keeps the feet warm when wet. Or paddlers' butts. Or treasure found on the river (as in river booty).

Bow -- The front of the boat. Or what a cocky paddler does when finished showing off. The paddle twirl is also an acceptable paddling bow.

Bracing (Brace) -- A technique using the paddle to stabilize the boat to prevent tipping; provides support similar to an outrigger on a sailboat. Sometimes accomplished by grabbing the gunwales in fear.

Broach -- Describes what happens when a canoe gets crosswise in the current and hangs on a rock. A common Odell Buckenflush maneuver. Or a way to commit canoe hara-kiri.

Bulkhead -- Sealed compartment in a canoe or kayak. Or a politically correct way to describe a "fathead".

Buzz bait -- A top water fishing lure that makes a whirring sound as it goes through the water. Or somebody sleeping in a boat when helicopters are nearby.

(C-1) or (C-2) -- See "Decked canoe"

Canoe -- A boat for people who can't kayak.

Canoe Roll -- A maneuver that turns a capsized canoe upright. Or a great name for a pastry.

Canuding -- The act of paddling a canoe, au-la-natural'. Not to be confused with Kayanuding or Raftnuding or Tubenuding; all lower-class versions of communing with nature.

Capsize -- When a boat tips over. Or a hat size, as in Big-Head-Fred's capsize is a bucket (as in buckethead).

Carabineer -- A mechanical piece of equipment that allows for quick attachment and release of rope or other objects used in climbing and/or river rescue. Or a device used to attach junk in boats. Or a device attached to a paddler's life jacket, which the paddler believes will help them appear to have a clue about what's happening. Or a cool key ring.

Catch -- The beginning phase of a canoe/kayak stroke just prior to the power phase when the paddle is positioned correctly. Or what folks who fall from their boats do with the throw-bag.

Class I, II, III, IV, V, VI -- Standard river classifications that denote the level of difficulty of rivers from "flat" to extreme "white" water. Or the elementary school grades.

Cockpit -- The enclosed central compartment of a kayak, in which the paddler sits. Or what old stored boats become (cockroach pits).

Combat Roll -- When a kayaker or canoeist completes a roll successfully after an unexpected flip in a river, not a swimming pool. Or when a GI tips the latrine of a superior officer with the officer still in the latrine.

Composite or Laminated -- Canoes that are built from some combination of different materials (fiberglass, Kevlar, carbon fiber). Or a term referring to a canoeist that reverts to the "dark side" and becomes a kayaker.

Crank bait -- A fishing lure that produces action when retrieved rather rapidly. Or an outdoors person who is constantly verbally abused by his or her spouse for being on the river only 50% of their free time.

Creek boat -- A type of kayak which is short and rounded on the ends and is designed to prohibit vertical pins in narrow creeks. Or any boat that can float in the streams of Arkansas.

Cruising Canoe -- A canoe design that is long, fast, has a low profile in the water and is not extremely maneuverable. Or any canoe utilized to pick up chicks.

Cross draw -- A crossover canoe stroke (an offside stroke) that turns or moves the boat to the opposite side from the side the paddle is on without changing the hand position. Or a canoe stroke that makes the paddler look like a barber pole.

Crown Land -- Canadian classification of Multiple-Use land, similar to land managed by the US Forest Service. Or a clown amusement park with a misspelled sign (Welcome to Crown Land).

Cubic feet per second (CFS) -- A measurement to describe the amount of water in an area at any given point in time. Or "a cold, frigging, suit" or "Canoe-fried in the sun," what happens to novice canoeists who don't use sun block.

D ring -- A ring used for attachment in canoes and rafts. Or a term used to describe a carabineer incorrectly.

Dead Fish Polo -- A game played by "sick" canoeists which consists of using a dead fish as the ball and paddles as the mallets. Goals are scored when the fish is "boated" (knocked into a canoe by a participant). The winner may eat the "ball" if desired. Face shots count extra. Sissies play the game using a sponge or water bottles as the ball.

Decked Canoe (C-1) or (C-2) -- A canoe that looks like a kayak but the boater is on his/her knees. Or a boat for people who double as a circus contortionist.

Deck Plate -- The triangular shaped top of a canoe at the stern and/or bow. Or a place under which to throw beer cans.

Depth -- The vertical measurement from the canoe hulls lowest point to its highest point from the ground. Or what most people feel when approaching their first class III rapid (or higher) when they are not ready for it, as in "out of my depth".

Directional Stability -- The ability of a watercraft to hold its course usually while moving. Or what an inebriated canoeist lacks.

Draw -- A paddle stroke used to turn or move the boat toward the paddle side. Or a term yelled by irate canoeing husbands when telling their wife what to do, after he screwed up.

Drop -- What happens when the river pours over a significant drop in elevation or obstruction, possibly forming a waterfall. (See waterfall-at least one hopes you see the waterfall).

Dry Bag -- Waterproof storage container (see Missouri Dry bag).

Dry suit -- A suit, which keeps the paddler dry when swimming rapids. Made of shoe-goo and duct tape. Sometime referred to as a high-tech weenie suit.

Duct Tape (Duck Tape) -- A wonder-substance used to repair everything. When in doubt, don't forget the duct tape.

Duffek Stroke (Hanging Draw Stroke) -- A turning paddle stroke where the boater leans out over the paddle, causing the craft to pivot around the paddle. Kind of like grabbing a pole while running at high speed, leaving your feet and swinging around.

Dugout Canoe -- An ancient canoe design where natives cut out or burned out portions of a tree trunk in forming a boat. Or what canoeists do when paddling in muddy areas.

Eddy -- A calm spot in the river caused by an obstruction where current flows upstream. A spot to relax, safe haven. Or Odell's cousin. Or a place many boaters tip over after the rough stuff.

Eddy line -- The transitional area between the eddy and the current. Or the search process for Odell's cousin, as in, "Got a line on Eddy?" Or what Cousin Eddy's fishing line is called. Or the line in the sand Odell drew with Cousin Eddy.

Eddy Turn -- A maneuver that drives the boat into an eddy and ends with the boat being positioned up stream, in the eddy. Or what Grandma always said after Odell did anything, "It's Eddy's turn."

Ender -- A maneuver performed in a kayak, C-1 and occasionally a canoe where the boat stands on end and is squirted perpendicularly upwards, out of a hole (kind of like spitting a water melon seed, straight up). Not to be confused with mooner.

Eskimo Roll -- See "Roll".

E'trier -- A rope or web ladder system devised to climb a rope. Always pronounced incorrectly by paddlers.

Expert -- A great paddler not in their local area. Or what Dr. Odell Buckenflush became when his wife determined he was no longer any fun when paddling. As in, "You were a lot of fun to paddle with until you became such a - - - -" expert!"

Farmer John Wetsuit -- A wetsuit design that has long legs and no sleeves. A smelly affair even in the best of times. Or an agriculture major suffering from incontinence.

Ferry -- A river maneuver used to go from one side of the river to the other without going downstream. Or a politically incorrect term describing a: paddler, kayaker, rafter, fisherman, civilian, county sheriff, Corps of Engineers Employee, or any other non-redneck.

Fiberglass -- A canoe material that is inexpensive and allows for a variety of shapes in boats. Or what one feels in their posterior when sliding or kneeling on old fiberglass watercraft.

Flare -- A term used to describe a watercraft that gets wider as it rises from the waterline to the gunwales. Or a piece of rescue equipment utilized 56 times with Dr. Odell Buckenflush.

Flat-water -- Any section of water that requires physical labor to make a boat move.

Floatation -- In whitewater, any type of improvised or purchased airbags that can be installed in watercraft to displace water. Or what obese individuals have built-in.

Freeboard -- The distance from the water surface to the gunwale of a canoe when the canoe is in water. This distance decreases with increased weight in the canoe. Or how most paddlers desire to eat when on long paddle trips.

Freestyle -- A form of canoe paddling on flat-water that involves improvisation, like ice dancing or floor exercises in gymnastics.

Gaskets -- A rubber device attached to dry suits that prohibit water from entering the suit at the neck, hands and/or feet. Or a type of hat as in "Head gasket." Or a defective birth control device.

Gorge -- A narrow valley-like constriction with deep cliffs that streams flow through. Known to have an appetite for boats.

Grab loop -- The short rope or handle attached to either end of a watercraft, most often used when carrying. Or what river rescue victims grasp when thrown a rope, prior to getting it tangled around their neck.

Gradient -- The amount a river drops during a given distance. Often an indicator of the river's difficulty. Also a good tip on what kind of shoes to bring as in high gradient = many portages.

Grip -- The end of a canoe or raft paddle. Or what novice and sometime veteran paddlers do to gunwales when fear overtakes skill and/or reason.

Greased lightning -- A "tad" quicker than lightening.

Guidebook -- A book providing river information like access points, safe water levels, ratings of rivers, privy locations, hot-dog stands, shoe stores, doctor's offices, gun shops and other information, most of which is forgotten as soon as one begins paddling.

Gunwales or gunnels -- The top rail or edge of a canoe usually grabbed in fear by passengers.

Hanging Draw Stroke -- (see Duffek Stroke)

Hatch -- The watertight area of a watercraft which is sealed by a hatch-cover. Or the last phase of human development for a C-1 boater. Not born of women but hatched from an egg.

Haystacks (Standing Waves) -- A series of big waves with easy paddling. May be rolled in (Or out of one's boat, into).

Helmet -- Protective headgear for those venturing onto whitewater or into the surf. Also used with paddlers who have a hard time standing on dry land.

Hole -- (Hydraulic or Keeper) A place in the river where water drops over an obstruction and is recirculated to form a potential danger of holding and keeping objects in the recirculating grip. Or what paddlers find in their floatation bags at the start of every boating season.

Hollow (Hollar, Holler) -- A geographic, hill-country description of a steep valley, gorge or drainage. Or the space inside a kayaker's head.

Horizon line -- A line across the river indicating a drop or ledge. See "waterfall" (at least we hope you see the waterfall).

Hull -- The body of a watercraft. Or an all-encompassing descriptive term, as in "he ate the hull thing."

Hydraulic -- (See "Hole"). A Hydraulic is often associated with man-made dams or weirs and is considered extremely dangerous. This is no place to play around.

Hyperthermia -- A serious medical condition in which person becomes overheated and ill. Or a hot time in the old town tonight.

Hypothermia -- A serious medical condition when a person gets very cold (falling into cold water) and loses the ability to function normally. Or a cold time in the old town tonight.

John boat -- An old style river boat which varied in length from 16 to 30 feet long and two to three feet wide. Or a floating portable toilet. Or a boat of owner's possession, e.g. Steve boat, Bill boat, Fred boat, etc.

Kayak or K-1 -- One-person boat for people who can't paddle a canoe.

Keel Line -- The longitudinal shape of the canoe's bottom. Or a great dessert... Keel Line Pie.

Keel Haul -- A technique used to punish bad and annoying paddlers where two ropes are tied to the paddler and they are drug the length of the canoe underwater. Works best with a War Canoe.

Keeper -- See "Hole" (At least we hope you see the hole).

Kneeling Pad(s) -- An optional though much-appreciated comfort item for canoeists; most are glued into their canoes. Use non-absorbent, waterproof, closed-cell foam; like the kind found in sleeping pads. Or what some paddlers wear as a fashion statement.

Kevlar -- A strong, light, fiber utilized in construction of canoes, airplanes and bulletproof vests. Soon all swat teams will be paddling bulletproof canoes.

Lead Boat -- The first boat in a group paddling together. Or a boat that sinks (Pb).

Leeward -- The side of a watercraft sheltered from the wind. Or how Southern boys usually lean.

Lifejacket -- (see PFD)

Line -- As in the line (route) of travel through a rapid. Or what paddlers form when standing in front of the privy prior to a major whitewater trip.

Lining -- The technique of moving ones unoccupied canoe up or downstream with ropes, usually around rapids. Avoids a portage. Or an adjective to describe a disreputable paddler, as in "That lining bastard!" Or a reference to the line at the privy "They be lining up."

List -- A tilt in a watercraft to the right (starboard) or left (port) usually caused by an unbalanced load. Or the gear and food planning inventory left at home by campers, fisherman and/or boaters.

Missouri Dry bag -- A five-gallon plastic bucket.

Moving water -- Any water that has current and is deep enough to get some floatable craft moving in it.

Offside -- The side of a canoe where one is not paddling. Or the side one usually wishes they were paddling on as they tip over. Or a five-yard penalty.

On side -- The preferred side of a canoe on which one paddles. Or how you want the lawman/woman to be at the takeout when he/she finds out you have alcoholic beverages in your canoe. "Hic, I'm suuure glad, you're on my side".

PFD -- Personal floatation device (life jacket, life vest). Or "pretty frigging dumb," if said after a poor run of a rapid.

Paddle -- The primary form of propulsion for canoes, kayaks, rafts and SUP. Or what locals sometimes do to boaters when found at their good fishing holes. Or a dated disciplinary technique used on all boaters at some time in their life.

Paddle Float -- An inflatable or foam device that assists in solo re-entry into a touring kayak from deep water. Or a blow-up doll placed on the end of a sea-kayak paddle for solo entry.

Paddle Leash -- A way to attach your paddle which allows you to keep track of it when you drop it, or stop to take photos, or pass out cookies.

Painters -- A line or rope tied to each end of a canoe usually causing more trouble than they are worth. This nautical term was derived from sailors hanging on a rope from the edge of a large ship and painting a name or picture on the ship. (Now you know the rest of the story).

Patagonia-Poster-Child -- A river clothing wardrobe consisting of clashing colors and high tech gear. Usually purchased either when on sale or by begging and whining for lower prices. Sometimes referred to as "Patagucchi."

Patagucchi -- (See "Patagonia-Poster-Child").

Pedestal (Saddle) -- A seat developed for paddling solo in a canoe; usually located in the middle of the boat and straddled by the paddler. (A tandem saddle allows two people to be seated). Yippy-yi-yo-ky-yay.

Peel out -- A river maneuver used to exit an eddy. Or a maneuver used with a vehicle when running a shuttle. Or exiting a wet suit.

Pillow -- A cushion of water striking a rock or obstruction that allows the boater to move over without pinning against it. Or a piece of paddling equipment utilized by many kayakers to alleviate hemorrhoids.

Poling -- A technique used to propel and maneuver canoes. Utilized mostly for upstream travel or when one forgets their paddles. Also a technique utilized by whitewater boaters when deciding to make a run over a hairy spot. "You gonna run it?" "I don't know, how about you?" "Let's take a poll and decide if we're gonna run this."

Pool -- Place where kayakers and some c-boaters proficiently roll their boats prior to going to moving water where they miss their roll. Also a place where fights tend to break out with people who think pools are for swimming rather than practicing kayak rolls.

Portage -- To carry your canoe rather than float it. A masochistic method of travel.

Power Face (of paddle blade) -- The part of the paddle blade in which force is applied. Or what a bad boss puts on in the morning.

Power Paddling -- Efficient method of boat propulsion (see Sit and Switch). Or what every male tandem canoeist will do to appear macho.

Prussic (Prussic knot) (Prusik) -- An efficient and strong knot used when tying a piece of rope into a loop. Used in assembly of rescue equipment. Or a Prussian marriage.

Pry (Push-away) -- A canoe stroke that moves or turns the boat away from the paddle side by using the paddle as a lever (crowbar) and the gunwale as the fulcrum. Or a method used on auto windows to obtain keys left in the shuttle vehicle.

Pump -- A hand pump helps get water out of canoes, kayaks, and/or rafts. Or what paddlers do to United States Army Corps of Engineers (USACE) to try to get them to release more water from the dam.

Put-in -- The place where paddlers begin a boating excursion (paddle trips usually end at the take-out). Or the first place available for paddlers to get wet.

Queer for gear -- A quality required of all American Canoe Association members who are trained in Swiftfwater Rescue. This trait is distinguished by an ability to rig the most elaborate rescue devices using available equipment, which is always carried by them. Or a boater that never misses equipment-swap-meet. Or an employee of any retail outdoor store, canoe store or backpacking store.

Raft -- A boat for people who can't do anything else.

Recovery -- A phase of the paddle stroke following the power phase in preparation for the next stroke. Or what weekend boaters do on Monday.

Rescue Rodeo -- A competition that usually takes place on rivers where teams of rescuers are challenged with scenarios requiring rescue.

Reverse Sweep Stroke -- A paddle stroke employed by the stern paddler that turns the boat toward the stern paddler's side. Or a technique employed in post-trip clean-up of vehicles where dirt is thrown back into the vehicle.

River Booty -- Gear or anything else found on the river, usually lost by other boaters. River Law is "finders' keepers". Or what is often viewed by the stern paddler when the bow partner's swimming suit is too small.

River Rodeo -- A competition that usually takes place on a large river wave where maneuvers and tricks are performed in kayaks or canoes. Or the Memphis Rodeo.

Roll (Eskimo roll) -- A kayak or canoe maneuver that turns a capsized boat upright. Or a move for those who can't keep their head out of the water.

Rooster tail -- A fishing lure that has a spinner, feathers and a treble hook (sometimes a single or tandem hook). Also a spurt of water in a rapid that shoots up like a broken water main. Or the tail of cock-a-doodle-do.

Royalex® (see ABS) -- Or a king/queen which has given up paddling (royal-ex).

Saddle -- (see pedestal)

Sea kayak -- A kayak designed for flat-water, coastal areas and tripping. Enclosed craft with storage bulkheads. Or a craft for whitewater boaters who have lost their cajones.

Self-Rescue -- What a paddler does to save themselves following a capsize. Or making the fateful decision to break-up with one's significant other.

Shaft -- The long skinny part of a canoe or kayak paddle. Or what the guy who is stuck with the worst paddling partner gets.

Shuttle -- The transporting of boats, vehicles, gear and people between the take-out and put-in on a river trip. (Sometimes referred to as a Cluster_-_-_-_).

Shuttle Bunny -- An individual who drives the shuttle for vehicle transfer during a paddle trip. This person usually doesn't paddle the river. More experienced Shuttle Bunnies will provide other services for paddlers, such as lunches, boat repair, and loading/unloading of gear. Occasionally these individuals have the audacity to ask for money for their services.

Sit-and-switch -- A canoe paddling technique where paddler switches sides in unison (one, two, three, hut). Or a hard to explain toileting technique.

Sit-on-Top Kayak -- A kayak designed for flat-water, coastal areas and tripping that is self-bailing and requires no spray skirt. Or a craft for whitewater boaters who have lost their cajones.

Sluice -- A constriction in the river where water pours over from three sides (kind of like being flushed down a toilet).

SPORT -- **S**tupid **P**eople **O**n **R**aft **T**rips.

Spray Skirt -- A neoprene or nylon skirt worn by a kayaker that attaches to the rim (coaming) of the cockpit to keep water out. Or a device that allows one to be a boating cross-dresser.

Squirt Boat -- A streamlined kayak utilized for river-rodeo maneuvers. Or what happens to any boat flushed through Bull Sluice on the Chattooga.

Stand Up Paddle Board (SUP) -- One of the more recent innovations in paddle sport where the paddler stands on a specially designed board (somewhat like a surfboard) and uses a longer paddle. Or a phrase used by homeys ("Sup?")

Standing Waves -- See "Haystacks".

Stern -- Rear of the boat. Or a place to put heavyweights. Or a paddler's gluteus maximus.

Strainer -- A dangerous obstruction (tree) in strong current. It may be located below, above, or on the surface of the river. **Never** go under strainers!

Surf (Surfing) (Surfing wave) -- A river maneuver where the paddler places the craft perpendicular to the wave, locking the boat in an upstream position, which allows the current to hold the boat in relatively the same place. Or an ocean wave battle ground for kayaks and traditional beach-bum types.

Swamp -- The act of unintentionally filling a boat with water. Or a destination that tourists are convinced to visit for paddling trips by Chamber of Commerce types.

Sweep Boat -- The last boat in a paddling group. Or the paddler suffering from Giardia.

Sweep Stroke -- A paddle stroke that turns the boat away from the paddle side. Or the technique employed in post-trip clean-up of vehicles.

Sweepers -- A low-hanging branch of a tree that tends to dislodge boaters that get too close as in "swept out of your boat and into the river". Or post-trip riders employed to clean up the shuttle vehicles.

Tag Line (snag line) -- A rescue technique where a rope is rigged to rescue a swimmer when their foot is entrapped. Or the card for a canoeist versus kayaker wrestling match.

Take Out -- The location where a paddle trip usually ends (trip begins at the put-in). Or what many paddlers wish was available after opening their soggy lunch bags.

Tandem -- Description for a two-person canoe, kayak, or raft. Sometimes referred to as: "Two dopes with hope in a boat."

Tennessee (or any state you put in this place) Wal-Mart -- A term used to denote a county trash drop. These have been established throughout the South as a benefit to environmental and river integrity.

Thar -- Anywhere that is not here. As in "over thar."

Thigh (knee) Braces -- Structures inside the cockpit of whitewater and touring kayaks that give the paddler important points of contact for boat control. Or what Forest Gump ran out of, as in "Run Forest Run!"

Throat -- Part of the paddle where the shaft meets the blade. Or a part of the human anatomy where a throw rope often hangs up.

Throwrope (Throw Rope) (Throw-Bag) -- A lifesaving rope enclosed in a nylon bag for throwing to victims in need of rescue. Rescuer hangs onto free end of rope (available in matching colors for PFD's). Often thrown incorrectly without hanging onto the end of the rope.

Thwart -- Wooden or aluminum cross-braces spanning side to side of a canoe (see yoke). Great to trip over when moving in the canoe.

Thwart Bag -- A bag that is attached to a thwart that is accessible to the paddler. This is a prime place to store oft-needed and illicit items.

Tie-Downs -- Ropes or webbing used to tie a boat to the car top boat racks. Boating etiquette suggests the boat owner be the person to tie the knots. Elastic/rubber tie downs are an accident waiting to happen.

Toll-Roll -- When one pays somebody to tip over another paddler. Not to be confused with "Troll-Roll" an event which happens when an unsuspecting paddler tips over for seemingly no reason, as in "the troll tipped me over."

Touring Canoe or Kayak -- A boat designed for long tripping. Or a whitewater boat for a tourist who wouldn't know the difference.

Tracking (Track) -- See *directional stability.*

Trim -- The way a boat rests in the water that is affected by the amount of weight in the craft. Or what many paddlers need to do in order to get into their wetsuits (trim down).

Troll-Roll -- An event which happens when an unsuspecting paddler tips over for seemingly no reason. "It must have been the River Troll rolling me over." Not to be confused with "Toll-roll" this is when one pays somebody to *tip over* another paddler.

Tumblehome -- A term used to describe a hull's cross-section. Or what many paddlers do at the takeout. Or a move describing the post-paddling-trip party.

Tump Line -- A strap that passes over the forehead and attaches to a portage pack. A harness for a human beast of burden.

Twin Otter -- A reliable twin engine workhorse airplane with a large cargo capacity. Twin otters have the ability to take off and land in a very short distance on land or water (an excellent shuttle craft). Or a phrase used to denote Siamese-twin-otters. Or a hill-country phrase as in, "That twin 'otter' get on 'outta' these parts."

Tyrolean crossing -- A rescue-rope-system used in climbing and river rescue scenarios where one traverses rivers or valleys while sitting in a harness. First developed by Hannibal in the Tyrolean Alps and used with elephants.

Vee or "V" -- A moving water formation resulting from obstructions. A **"V"** pointed at you indicates a rock while a **"V"** pointed away from you indicates safe passage. Or the "victory sign" given after a successful bowel cleansing prior to a paddle trip.

Volume -- A term used to describe the capacity of a hull shape. Also used to denote the amount of water in a given river. Or the term used to describe the amount of water that always gets in a white-water open canoe. Or what the bow paddler should turn up when speaking while paddling white water.

War Canoe -- Oversized canoe used to transport many people. Often used in competitions. Or a big-ass boat. Or a boat for big asses.

Waterfalls -- What water does when it goes over a drop.

Waterline -- The point to which the water rises on a boat's hull when the boat is loaded. Or a damp throw rope.

Waves -- A change in the surface of water that occurs as water moves and is usually created by wind, tides, drops in gradient, and/or people hitting the water. Or what people do to folks in need of rescue when they have no throw rope.

Wet Suit -- A skintight neoprene suit made in different designs which keep paddlers warm by holding a small amount of water between the suit and the body. It also keeps paddlers cold until they fall into the water.

Wet exit -- Coming out of a capsized canoe/kayak. Or falling out of the shower.

White water -- Rapidly moving and turbulent water on a river. The International Classification scale consists of: Class I through Class VI. Class II and above may be considered white water. Flushing the toilet is probably Class III.

Yoke -- A type of sculpted center thwart that allows one to portage (carry) a canoe more easily across their shoulders. Allows the person carrying the canoe to become *oxen for the day*.

Z-Drag -- A rescue device used to unpin boats. It provides a mechanical advantage made with ropes and **carabineers** (like a come-a-long). Or what everyone does with their boat in times of low water.

APPENDIX:

The Odell Buckenflush Chronicles Adding to the River Tales

APPENDIX 1:
RIVERS AND GEOGRAPHIC
AREAS MENTIONED IN TALES

Baja California, Bay of LA, Mexico- **BORDER CROSSING, SOUTH!** Ch. 1.

Barren Lake, Kentucky- **ODELL BUCKENFLUSH'S BEST CANOE PURCHASE**, Ch. 2.

Boulder River, Montana- **TAKE THE NEXT TURN, RIGHT?** Ch. 4.

Boundary Waters, Minnesota- **THE GLASS RUNNETH OVER**, Ch. 4.

Boston Mountains, Arkansas - **ORIGINATION OF RIVERS IN BOSTON MOUNTAINS, ARKANSAS,** Prolog.

Buffalo River, Arkansas- **ORIGINATION OF RIVERS IN BOSTON MOUNTAINS, ARKANSAS,** Prolog; **EDGE EFFECT**, Ch. 2; **HACKY SACK HEAD**, Ch. 3.

Chattooga River, Georgia- **BULL SLUICE MOOSE CALL**, Ch. 1; **IMPROVISE AND ADJUST**, Ch. 4.

Chicago, Illinois- **THE GLASS RUNNETH OVER**, Ch. 4.

Clear Creek, Tennessee- **NIGHT HIKE**, Ch. 3.

Cumberland River (Big South Fork), Tennessee & Kentucky- **CARTOON FALL**, Ch. 3.

Drakes Creek, Kentucky- **HANGIN' WITH THE BUCKENFLUSHES,** Ch. 2; **HOW LOW CAN YOU GO?** Ch. 3.

Finley River, Missouri- **THE LOANER BOAT,** Ch. 1; **FINLEY RIVER BAPTISM,** Ch. 2; **CHLORDANE SUCKERS,** Ch. 2.; **DO IT AGAIN DADDY,** Ch. 2

Ft. Benton, Montana- **ONE TOUGH TOWN,** Ch. 4.

Gardiner, Montana- **TAKE THE NEXT TURN, RIGHT?** Ch. 4.

Green River, Kentucky- **SNAKE SHOCK,** Ch. 3.

Idaho Potato Museum- **THE GLASS RUNNETH OVER,** Ch. 4.

Jacks Fork River, Missouri- - **THE LOST BOAT,** Ch. 2; **BRUTE FORCE WILL GET YOU NOWHERE,** Ch. 4.

James River, Missouri- **ROPES---WHO NEEDS THEM?** Ch. 1; **POLE OR PADDLE?** Ch. 2; **CHLORDANE SUCKERS,** Ch. 2.

Jasper, Arkansas- **THE GLASS RUNNETH OVER,** Ch. 4.

Kings, River, Arkansas- **ORIGINATION OF RIVERS IN BOSTON MOUNTAINS, ARKANSAS,** Prolog.

Lake Placid, New York- **THE CANOE LUGE,** Ch. 1.

Louisville, Kentucky- **ROBBED!** Ch. 4.

Mammoth Cave National Park, Kentucky- **SNAKE SHOCK,** Ch. 3.

Mississippi River, Missouri- **THE SOAP BOX CANOE,** Ch. 1; **THE FLOOD OF 93';** Ch. 3.

Missouri River, Montana- **ONE TOUGH TOWN**, Ch. 4.

Mulberry River, Arkansas- **SHUTTLE RUNNER DEJAVU'**, Ch. 3.

Nantahala River, North Carolina- **PADDLE LA PIEU'**, Ch. 1.

Nuevo Progresso, Texas- **BORDER CROSSING, SOUTH!** Ch. 1.

Obed-Emory systems in Tennessee- **EVERYBODY RIDES ABOVE THIS WHITEWATER**, Ch. 1; **NIGHT HIKE**, Ch. 3.

Obey River (West Fork), Tennessee- **SHE-RAFT,** Ch. 1.

Ocoee River, Tennessee- **LOCKED WHEN LOADED**, Ch. 2.

Piney River, Arkansas- **NOGGIN KNOCKER**, Ch. 3; **YOU CAN'T DEFEAT THE RIVER**, Ch. 4.

Quetico Provincial Park, Ontario, Canada- **BORDER CROSSING**, Ch. 4.

Russell, Kansas- **THIS IS KANSAS, DORTHY**, Ch. 2.

Spanish River, Ontario, Canada- **HOW NOT TO POOP IN THE WOODS**, Ch. 3.

St. Louis, Missouri- **THE SOAP BOX CANOE**, Ch. 1; **THE FLOOD OF 93'**; Ch. 3.

Sault St. Marie, Michigan- **BORDER CROSSING... REVISITED**, Ch. 4.

Sea of Cortez- **BORDER CROSSING, SOUTH!** Ch. 1.

APPENDIX 2:
PREVIOUSLY PUBLISHED
VERSIONS OF TALES

BULL SLUICE MOOSE CALL. Ozark Mountain Paddler 12-93.

THE CANOE LUGE. Tennessee Scenic River Association Watershed #324, 11-95.

THE SOAP BOX CANOE. Tennessee Scenic River Association Watershed, 7-95, No.332. Ozark Paddler, 1-96, and Southern Kentucky Paddler, 3-96

THE FLYING FORTRESS SLUICE. Tennessee Scenic River Association Watershed, 9-97.

CLOSE CALL. Paddler 2-98.

APPENDIX 3 :
SUBJECT INDEX

The **subject index** identifies tales by topic.

Children-raising-boating with-fishing with- survival
PACKING OBSESSION, Ch. 1
THIS IS KANSAS, DOROTHY, Ch. 2
HANGIN' WITH THE BUCKENFLUSHES', Ch. 2
AMPHIBIAN ENEMA, Ch. 2
DO IT AGAIN DADDY Ch. 2
FLOATERS AND SINKERS, CH. 4
ONE TOUGH TOWN, Ch. 4

Death, Dying, and Close Calls
ROPES--- WHO NEEDS THEM? , CH. 1
THE SOAP BOX CANOE, Ch. 1
THIS IS KANSAS, DOROTHY, Ch. 2
DO IT AGAIN DADDY Ch. 2
THE DARWIN AWARD FOR CAMPING, CH. 3
SHUTTLE RUNNER DEJA VU, Ch. 3

Ethics – Doing the Right Thing-Making the correct choice
BULL SLUICE MOOSE CALL, Ch. 1
THE LOST BOAT, Ch. 2
FINLEY RIVER BAPTISM, CH. 2
CHLORDANE SUCKERS, Ch. 2
ROBBED! , Ch. 4

Firearms-Archery-Hunting
ODELL BUCKENFLUSH'S BEST CANOE PURCHASE, Ch. 2
BORDER CROSSING, Ch. 4

Fires- usage- LNT Principles
THE DARWIN AWARD FOR CAMPING, CH. 3

Fishing
HANDS-FREE ALPHA MALE, CH. 1
CHLORDANE SUCKERS, Ch. 2
TAKE THE NEXT TURN, RIGHT? , Ch.

BORDER CROSSING... REVISITED, Ch. 4
THE DOING: OVER AND OVER...EPILOG

Love and Affection
THE GLASS RUNNETH OVER, Ch. 4

Medical Emergency-Wilderness First Responder-Backcountry Emergency
A VISIT TO THE DARK SIDE, Ch. 2
HACKY SACK HEAD, CH. 3
THE DARWIN AWARD FOR CAMPING, CH. 3

Paddle skills, Techniques, Maneuvers
ORIGINATION OF RIVERS IN BOSTON MOUNTAINS, ARKANSAS, PROLOG
PADDLE LA PIEU', Ch. 1
THE LOST BOAT, Ch. 2
A VISIT TO THE DARK SIDE, Ch. 2
THE FLOOD OF 93', Ch. 3
NOGGIN' KNOCKER, Ch. 3
BRUTE FORCE WILL GET YOU NOWHERE, Ch. 4
IMPROVISE AND ADJUST, Ch. 4
YOU CAN'T DEFEAT THE RIVER, Ch. 4

Recycle-Reuse-River Booty
THE LOANER BOAT, Ch. 1
THE LOST BOAT, Ch. 2

Rescue
THE LOANER BOAT, Ch. 1
THE LOST BOAT, CH. 2,
THE EDGE EFFECT, CH. 2
THIS IS KANSAS, DOROTHY, Ch. 2
NIGHT HIKE, Ch. 3
THE FLOOD OF 93', Ch. 3
TECHNOLOGY CONUNDRUM, Ch. 3

THE VOYAGEUR, Ch. 1
PACKING OBSESSION, Ch. 1
THIS IS KANSAS, DOROTHY, Ch. 2
AMPHIBIAN ENEMA, Ch. 2
NIGHT HIKE, Ch. 3
TECHNOLOGY CONUNDRUM, Ch. 3
BORDER CROSSING, Ch. 4
THE GLASS RUNNETH OVER, Ch. 4
TAKE THE NEXT TURN, RIGHT? , Ch.
BORDER CROSSING... REVISITED, Ch. 4

APPENDIX 4:
CHARACTER INDEX

The **Character Index** identifies which characters are in each tale. Because Dr. Odell Buckenflush is in each tale, his name is omitted

BUCKENFLUSH TALES CHARACTERS

Buckenflush Sr. (Odell's Dad) - **ODELL BUCKENFLUSH'S BEST CANOE PURCHASE,** Ch. 2.

Bezel Buckenflush - **THE LOST BOAT,** Ch. 2; **ROPES- WHO NEEDS THEM?** Ch. 1;
EDGE EFFECT, Ch. 2; **CHLORDANE SUCKERS,** Ch. 2

James David Buckenflush - **SHE-RAFT,** Ch. 1; **THE FLYING FORTRESS SLUICE,** Ch. 2

Jayrell Buckenflush - **EVERYBODY RIDES ABOVE THIS WHITEWATER,** Ch. 1; **THIS IS KANSAS DOROTHY,** Ch. 2; **LOCKED WHEN LOADED!** Ch. 2; **FINLEY RIVER BAPTISM,** Ch. 2; **HANGIN' WITH THE BUCKENFLUSHES,** Ch. 2; **EDGE EFFECT,** Ch. 2; **DO IT AGAIN DADDY,** Ch. 2; **FLOATERS AND SINKERS,** Ch. 4

Lulu Belle Buckenflush - **THE SOAP BOX CANOE,** Ch. 1; **EVERYBODY RIDES ABOVE THIS WHITEWATER,** Ch. 1, **THIS IS KANSAS DOROTHY,** Ch. 2; **LOCKED WHEN LOADED!** Ch. 2; **FINLEY RIVER BAPTISM,** Ch. 2; **HANGIN' WITH THE BUCKENFLUSHES** Ch. 2; **BRACING ON THE DROP** Ch. 2; **EDGE EFFECT,** Ch. 2; **ODELL BUCKENFLUSH'S BEST CANOE PURCHASE,** Ch. 2; **NOGGIN KNOCKER,** Ch. 3; **ROBBED!** Ch. 4; **THE GLASS RUNNETH OVER,** Ch. 4; **DO IT AGAIN DADDY,** Ch. 2

Mom Buckenflush - **PACKING OBSESSION,** Ch. 1

Tyrell Buckenflush - **THIS IS KANSAS DOROTHY,** Ch. 2; **LOCKED WHEN LOADED!** Ch. 2; **FINLEY RIVER BAPTISM,** Ch. 2; **HANGIN' WITH THE BUCKENFLUSHES,** Ch. 2; **AMPHBIAN ENEMA,** Ch. 2; **EDGE EFFECT,** Ch. 2; **A VISIT TO THE DARK SIDE,** Ch. 2; **DO IT AGAIN DADDY,** Ch. 2; **FLOATERS AND SINKERS;** Ch. 4

Dr. Joe Giant - **BRUTE FORCE WILL GET YOU NOWHERE,** Ch. 4

Grandma Gibbons - **BULL SLUICE MOOSE CALL,** Ch. 1

Hosehead Grey - **EVERYBODY RIDES ABOVE THIS WHITEWATER** Ch. 1; **HACKY SACK HEAD,** Ch. 3; **HOW NOT TO POOP IN THE WOODS,** Ch. 3; **THE GLASS RUNNETH OVER,** Ch. 4

Jim Grey (Loyal Buckenflush companion) - **EVERYBODY RIDES ABOVE THIS WHITEWATER,** Ch. 1; **NIGHT HIKE,** Ch. 3; **HACKY SACK HEAD,** Ch. 3; **HOW' NOT TO POOP IN THE WOODS,** Ch. 3; **THE GLASS RUNNETH OVER,** Ch. 4

Stu Hole – **PADDLE LA PIEU',** Ch. 1; **THE LOANER BOAT,** Ch. 1; **NIGHT HIKE,** Ch. 3; **HACKY SACK HEAD,** Ch. 3; **TAKE THE NEXT TURN RIGHT,** Ch. 4

Jon Nitrus – **BULL SLUICE MOOSE CALL,** Ch. 1; **EVERYBODY RIDES ABOVE THIS WHITEWATER,** Ch. 1; **SHE-RAFT,** Ch. 1; **THE VOYAGEUR,** Ch. 1; **PADDLE LA PIEU',** Ch. 1; **NIGHT HIKE,** Ch. 3; **HACKY SACK HEAD,** Ch. 3; **TECHNOLOGY CONUNDRUM,** Ch. 3; **IMPROVISE AND ADJUST,** Ch. 4

Mike Oldnose - **THE FLYING FORTRESS SLUICE,** Ch. 2

Auburn Redd – **EVERYBODY RIDES ABOVE THIS WHITEWATER, Ch. 1; THE GLASS RUNNETH OVER,** Ch. 4

Dead Ted Redd – **EVERYBODY RIDES ABOVE THIS WHITEWATER, Ch. 1; PADDLE LA PIEU', Ch. 1; NIGHT HIKE, Ch. 3; HACKY SACK HEAD, Ch. 3; SNAKE SHOCK,** Ch. 3; **NOGGIN KNOCKER,** Ch. 3; **TECHNOLOGY CONUNDRUM,** Ch. 3; **IMPROVISE AND ADJUST, Ch. 4; THE GLASS RUNNETH OVER,** Ch. 4; **BORDER CROSSING- REVISITED,** Ch. 4

Willy Joe Wiley- **HANDS-FREE ALPHA MALE, Ch. 1; EDGE EFFECT,** Ch. 2; **ODELL BUCKENFLUSH'S BEST CANOE PURCHASE** Ch. 2

WHAT KIND OF PERSON
WOULD WRITE THIS STUFF?

Steve Spencer is a professor in the School of Kinesiology, Recreation and Sport at Western Kentucky University and the founder of the Outdoor Leadership Program at WKU, a 25+ year old program in experiential education. He is an instructor trainer with the American Canoe Association and a Leave No Trace Master Educator. He enjoys a wide variety of outdoor pursuits but is master of very few. He has been truly blessed and views his as a "lifetime of play" and the glass is always half full, not half empty.

Steve and his wife **Debby Spencer** reside in Bowling Green, KY. The Spencer's have travelled and paddled throughout North America. With family roots in the Ozark Mountains, both hold degrees from the University of Arkansas (Go Hogs!), Mizzou, and Missouri State. In a former lifetime, Steve spent 12 years coaching football.

Debby Spencer is the President of *We Make Things Happen*, a company that works in tourism and economic development http://www.wmthcorp.com/ and http://www.trailsrus.com/. She served as inspiration and backboard for the Odell Buckenflush Chronicles.

Beau and Tyler Spencer both graduated from Western Kentucky University and each have contributed to illustrations and editorial insight in the Odell Buckenflush Chronicles. Beau is in the U.S. Air Force and Tyler is currently working toward a PhD in Sport Administration.

John Lee, another Western Kentucky University graduate, did much of the original artwork for the Buckenflush Tales.

Tom Foster, provided the illustration for *This is Kansas, Dorothy.* He is a retired graphics designer for the Public Broadcasting Service at Western Kentucky University. He has published illustrations in children's instructional books and experienced the joys of canoeing white water.

WHAT FOLKS ARE SAYING ABOUT THE ODELL BUCKENFLUSH CHRONICLES

"Bathroom reading is definitely an important genre and the pages of this book fills the niche in more ways than one…."
Dr. Larry Snider,
Dean of Potter College of Arts and Letters,
Western Kentucky University

"These tales are perfect "can" reading!"
Willy Joe Wiley

Really? A book only about paddling?
Marquis de Sade

"I ain't dead, yet!"
Dead Ted Redd

"These tales are just the right length for my time on the pot."
Gary Sims

Check out
Odellbuckenflush.com

Made in the USA
Monee, IL
09 October 2023

44268022R00104